Theonomics

Reconnecting Economics with Virtue and Integrity

EDITED BY

ANDREW LIGHTBOWN & PETER SILLS

Sacristy
Press

Sacristy Press
PO Box 612, Durham, DH1 9HT

www.sacristy.co.uk

First published in 2014 by Sacristy Press, Durham

Sacristy Limited, registered in England & Wales, number 7565667

British Library Cataloguing-in-Publication Data
A catalogue record for the book is available from the British Library

ISBN 978-1-908381-18-7

THE AUTHORS

Richard Backhouse read Economics at Selwyn College, Cambridge, with the sincere intention of becoming a journalist. Initially distracted by the possibility of a PhD, he became a teacher 'by accident'. After stints at Oundle School and Bradfield College, where he was Head of Economics, Director of Pastoral and Extra-Curricular Activities, and a Housemaster, he was appointed as Principal of Monkton Combe School in 2005, where he enjoys the challenge of leading a school which is both Christian and in the mainstream of the British Public School tradition.

Nick Bion joined the company his father started shortly after leaving university over 30 years ago. The company, which he now largely owns and manages, is a specialist in sheet metal processing, employing 30 people with a turnover of about £4M. The company and its employees contribute to society both in terms of the products they manufacture, and tax revenues and charity payments totalling over £1M. The company is very focused on adding value to its customers, and sees profits as one measure of its successful operation.

Frank Canosa is a Visiting Professor at the University of Buckingham, where he has taught post-graduate courses in corporate finance, the international financial system, and international financial regulation and anti-money laundering. He has also taught wealth management for EDHEC Business School, France, the Cass Business School, City University, and the British Bankers' Association. Frank is a Chartered Fellow of the Chartered Institute for Securities & Investment (CISI), and its Chief Continuing Professional Development Adviser; he is also Special Adviser to the Board of Newton Investment Management Ltd., and formerly CEO of Julius Baer International Ltd. Before his career in wealth management, Frank was an investment banker at Bank of America International Ltd. where he was Executive Director in charge of capital markets and corporate finance. Born in Havana, Cuba he is married with two adult daughters, and holds dual British and American nationality.

Keith Croxton has been a Trustee Director of *Chapter 1 Housing Association* since 1996. Prior to that, he was a career civil servant with the Department of Health and Social Security, and, immediately before moving to *Chapter 1*, was the Area Director for Merseyside for the Benefits Agency. Keith is married to Gill, and has two daughters and four grandchildren.

Nick Fane has been a teacher, education officer, and local government executive, often involved in the complex issues of allocating financial and other resources across competing social and political priorities. He is a qualified counsellor, and is currently a volunteer with a hospital chaplaincy. He is married to Sue, with a daughter, two sons, and two grandsons.

Alan Hargrave was born in a terraced house in the middle of Leeds—an area now buried under university buildings and an inner city motorway. He trained as a Chemical Engineer before working for ten years with the Anglican Church in South America, first on an economic development project with indigenous people in northern Argentina, then lecturing in Industrial Microbiology and working with the Church in Bolivia. He returned to the UK in 1987 to train as a priest. In 1994 he became the first vicar of a new parish on a council estate on the edge of Cambridge. In 2004 he became Canon Missioner of Ely Cathedral. He is the author of *An Almighty Passion*, illustrating the great doctrines of God with stories from ordinary life, and *Living Well*, a guide to finding a Rule of Life.

Rosie Harper was born in London, and grew up in Norwich. She is both British and Swiss. After graduating from Birmingham

University, she undertook post-graduate studies at the Royal Academy of Music, and worked as professional singer. After further studies, including an MA in Philosophy and Religion, Rosie was ordained, and now serves as the vicar of Great Missenden and as Chaplain to the Bishop of Buckingham. She is a Canon of Christ Church, Oxford, and chair of the Oxford Nandyal Education Foundation, a charity focussed on capacity building in rural Indian schools. She is also a member of the General Synod, and committed to working for issues of justice and equality within and beyond the church.

Andrew Lightbown was ordained deacon in 2013, and serves in the Schorne team of parishes in Buckinghamshire. Andrew has an MBA, and, before ordination, he worked for many years in the city of London, where he gained extensive experience of the financial services industry, and was Managing Director (Retail) of Old Mutual Asset Managers UK. From there, he moved to the University of Buckingham where he lectured in Business and Business Ethics. Andrew is actively involved with two of the organizations profiled in Part Two: Quicken Trust and *Chapter 1 Housing Association*. He is an oblate of Alton Abbey, married with two daughters, and, aside from theology and economics, enjoys walking the dog and skiing, and is a passionate fan of Northampton Saints Rugby Club.

Peter Sills was born in north London, and after an initial career teaching law at Kingston University, during which he was called to the Bar, he was ordained in 1981. He served in three parishes in south London before being appointed a Canon of Ely Cathedral, where he was Vice-Dean from 2003 to 2008. Peter's interest in the public aspects of faith and in Benedictine spirituality led to the foundation of the Ely Business Ethics Forum, which has since morphed into the Ely Cathedral Business Group. He gained his PhD in 2000 for a study of the ethics of the privatization of natural monopoly industries in the UK, and his publications include *The Time Has Come*, a Lenten journey through St Mark's gospel, *Your*

Kingdom Come, reflections on faith, justice and hope, and the Scala Souvenir Guide to Ely Cathedral. Now retired, Peter continues his Benedictine work from his home in Sussex.

Alan Wilson was born in Edinburgh and grew up in London and Kent. After studies at St John's College Cambridge and doctoral research at Balliol College Oxford in historical theology, he was ordained in the Church of England. He has served as a parish priest in Reading and Sandhurst, and as a prison chaplain, before becoming Bishop of Buckingham in 2003. He takes a special interest in new media, writes a blog, and is Chair of the Oxford Diocesan Board of Education.

PREFACE

'Where are we going?' For several years now it has been apparent, even if officially unacknowledged, that generally accepted economic ideas are not working. Economically the world is depressed, and no one seems really to know what to do. The contributors to this book do not believe that we have all the answers, but we do believe that any effective answer involves taking seriously the insights of the Christian faith. Economic crises are nothing new, but the present crisis has a new dimension. It has laid bare the shallow ethics of major financial institutions, and, by implication, other aspects of commercial life also. Economic hardship is compounded by anger and disgust. Important economic institutions seem to have cut loose from decency and truth. All religions have something to offer in this situation, and the Christian faith in particular has rich resources that enable us to reconnect economics with ethics and integrity. This book examines some of those resources and offers examples of successful businesses and other organizations where they have been put into effect. It is written for the general reader, for anyone who senses that there is a missing dimension in the solutions so far offered for getting the economy back on track. It is written in the belief that economics needs a new approach.

'Theonomics' is what we have called this new approach—not a word you will find in the dictionary. It is our shorthand term for an approach to economics that is shaped by the insights, the teaching and the ethics of the Christian faith. Theonomics is a response to deficiencies in the way we think about economics today. These deficiencies are serious; most obviously they underlie the economic crisis that began in 2008, but more fundamentally they point to the limited theoretical basis of economic concepts and institutions. The genesis of this book was the work of Andrew Lightbown, who through his work, church, and other contacts became aware of a group of people who, in various ways, were endeavouring to shape their work according to the insights of their Christian faith. From the outset the aim was not simply to present a theoretical or theological account of what a theonomic approach to economic issues might look like, but, more importantly, to ground it in practical experience. As the project took shape, Andrew met Peter Sills, who had time on his hands and the same desire to connect faith and work, and invited him to be his co-editor. Since Andrew began training for ordination in 2011, Peter has overseen the project and brought it to completion.

The plan of the book follows Andrew's original outline, and falls into two parts. The first five chapters set out some basic Christian principles and insights for evaluating economic life and its challenges, and the last seven chapters describe in a practical way the experience of those who are endeavouring to use those principles and insights in the day-to-day business of earning a living. As will be seen from the list of authors, the contributors come from a wide variety of backgrounds and experience. They come from different traditions within the Church, and our aim has been not to harmonise their contributions into a single approach, but rather to let each distinctive voice speak for itself.

In the Foreword Martyn Percy, recently appointed as Dean of Christchurch, Oxford, places the study in the context of the Gospel story and the teaching of Jesus, noting that from the first (drawing on its roots in Judaism) Christianity has been 'an inherently political, economically active, and profoundly social faith.' In Chapter 1 Andrew Lightbown takes up the theme, setting out some of the underlying issues of the present crisis and describing the basic tenets of the theonomic approach. He describes the ethical deficit and the spiritual poverty of modern life, and points to the way in which economic thinking has become divorced from the social realities in which it should be rooted. Theonomics, he argues, offers a way back through the pursuit of virtue, justice, and integrity. The stress on these values is important because theonomics is not a new body of theory; it accepts the free market as the most efficient, if flawed, way of organizing economic life, but recognises that the way the market works is not ethically neutral.

Those who operate in the market bring to their work certain values and attitudes which shape what they do and the way that they do it. Often these values are implicit, taken for granted, and not thought through, but they provide the moral framework within which economic activity takes place. Theonomics is about changing that framework; it is about rethinking the moral landscape and questioning some of the implicit values and attitudes that shape it. So, in Chapter 2, Peter Sills offers a Christian framework for economics. Drawing on biblical and Christian social teaching, he identifies six main values around which the framework is built: community, solidarity, justice, gift, service and subsidiarity. He also introduces the teaching of St Benedict of Nursia, a sixth century monk whose influence in the Church has been huge but remains largely unknown. His teaching, particularly about the core virtue of humility, resonates with many people today, both within and without the Church. However, identifying the right values is not enough; equally important is letting them become part of us, so that they become the implicit, taken-for-granted, day-to-day values of economic life. In Chapter 3 Alan Hargrave shows a way in which this can be done. Continuing the Benedictine theme, he takes the three monastic vows of obedience, stability and conversion of life, and shows how they are the key to the inner growth and change that can transform both our personal and working lives—as he says, the vows offer a 'framework for flourishing'.

One of the basic Christian convictions is that people are more important than systems, and this shapes the theonomic conception of value, considered by Rosie Harper and Alan Wilson in Chapter 4. Modern economic calculation exalts financial value over human value; people tend to be seen merely as economic units whose worth is determined by their wealth or usefulness, and one result is that people are described as consumers: we are defined by our appetites and not by our humanity. This is, of course, in sharp contrast to the teaching of Jesus, and impoverishes rich and poor alike. Economic calculation needs to be recalibrated if the economy is to serve the needs of all. Concluding Part One, in Chapter 5 Richard Backhouse reflects on the nature of trust, an underpinning necessity of all transactions which the banking crisis has severely damaged.

Part Two illustrates the themes of Part One with some specific examples of how a theonomic approach might work out in practice. Economically, much depends on the quality of leadership, especially so in times of crisis. Leaders set the values, the tone, and the direction of an organization, and the present crisis is very much a crisis of leadership. Thus Part Two begins, in Chapter 6, with an examination of the Benedictine approach to leadership which has much practical wisdom to offer. Starting with the perception that ethics can impede a successful career, Peter Sills argues that the financial crisis has more to do with inadequate ethical standards and wrong judgements, i.e. a lack of inner, personal controls, than inadequate external controls and regulatory systems. To counter this he sets out a model of ethical, virtuous leadership, designed to strengthen a leader's inner resources. In Chapter 7 Andrew Lightbown and Nick Fane draw on their experience of Quicken Trust, a charity that works to relieve poverty in Uganda, to challenge the narrowness of an economic system that has no place for gift transactions, only recognising and dealing with things of monetary value. Arguing for an understanding of charity as the voluntary redistribution of valued assets inspired by the Gospel principle of agape (generous self-giving in love, both materially and spiritually), they show how gift is another medium of exchange capable of dramatically increasing well-being, and which challenges the basis of accepted economic theory. In Chapter 8, Investment, Frank Canosa takes John Wesley's injunction in matters of commerce to 'preserve the spirit of a healthful mind', and asks what this means in the context of ethical investment. While there is wide agreement about investments to avoid—companies dealing in armaments, pornography, tobacco and alcohol, which support oppressive regimes, or have a poor environmental record—he notes that there is a growing positive approach of seeking companies which aim to enhance the environment and the well-being of staff, customers and the wider society. The right use of wealth to promote socially and environmentally responsible goals undergirds the theonomic framework.

Nick Bion in Chapter 9, Work, writing from his experience in running a sheet metal processing company, asks what are the responsibilities of corporate ownership? Too often ownership is seen in terms of capital gain—building up the company to sell it on, maximising revenue and shareholder value, and minimising tax payments. Nick sets out a different approach in which obligations to customers, suppliers, staff, and (through the tax system) society are fully and willingly honoured. When these values are added to a company 'culture' that actively seeks openness in decision-making and a work ethic that promotes personal growth, we have an excellent example of what a theonomic framework can achieve. An example of similar principles applied to a social sector of the economy is given in Chapter 10 by Keith Croxton who writes about The Housing Conundrum. How do we help someone at the bottom of the social scale, who has no place to live, to find the security that is a home? Being clear that simply providing a house is not the complete answer is the starting point: a home is more than a house; among other things it requires a community to give it context, identity and security. Drawing on the work of *Chapter 1 Housing Association*, Keith illustrates a Christian approach to resolving the housing conundrum. Part Two concludes with Chapter 11, School for the Lord's Service, in which Richard Backhouse discusses the aims and methods of education from the perspective of a modern faith school. Starting with the observation that 'the mind is not a vessel to be filled, but a fire to be kindled', he asks what a school would look like if the institution were to seek to embed the Christian faith in its workings at the deepest level. Among other things, the value of each child would displace measures of educational output as the school's primary concern; education in personal qualities and values (might we say virtues?) would displace 'educating young people in a manner reflective of contemporary culture.'

Finally, in an Afterword Peter Sills offers a personal reflection on the issues that we have addressed.

We see this book as a work in progress, and would welcome further contributions. We would particularly welcome further contributions to Part Two, examples of a theonomic approach to other aspects of the economy, for example, farming, retail, insurance, banking, and health care. We know that our concerns are shared by those of other faiths and indeed by those whose faith is not expressed religiously; if your concerns resonate with ours, we should be glad to hear from you.

Andrew Lightbown & Peter Sills

FOREWORD: THEONOMICS?

How are Christians supposed to engage with the world when they are, in truth, expecting a new world that is yet to come? Why bother with the temporal when minds and hearts are meant to be fixed on the eternal? What can theology offer the churches to help Christians of all persuasions maintain their poise and prophetic witness within a public and plural world? These questions pepper the pages of the New Testament as much as they have absorbed Christians for two millennia.

On the one hand, Christians are called out of the world, and are to no longer regard themselves as belonging to it. On the other hand, they are to be engaged with the world in all its complexities and ambiguities as fully as possible: to be salt, light and yeast in society, incarnating the life of Christ into the breadth of humanity. The apparent dilemma is expressed by by one early Christian writer (the unknown author of the late second-century Epistle to Diognetus) who speaks of Christians living as citizens and aliens in every land where they reside. They belong to the people and places they reside in, and are subject to the laws and governments they are under, but they also belong to another kingdom. In short, every home to Christians is, in some sense, foreign, for Christians seek a kingdom that is to come.

The unknown author expresses a paradox that is at the heart of Christian engagement with social ordering, the politics, economics and public life.[1] He or she speaks for the first generation of Christians as much for those of the twenty-first, by formulating the sense of divided loyalties that can sometimes threaten the very identity of the church, and the place of Christians within the world.

The contributions of the Editors and Authors of *Theonomics* are to be warmly welcomed at this time. For money, and the economy, remain central concerns of social and public life—not just at national levels, but also as one of the defining issues of international affairs and global issues. How to view debt, how to create and share wealth, and what our responsibilities are to the poor are always major Christian concerns. Make no mistake: money matters.

The challenge—with all its possibilities and problems—of how to understand and imagine our economic systems, to reflect upon and utilize money (its potential for good, and for evil), is never far from the heart of the Christian gospel. Yet Jesus' attitude to money was highly ambivalent. On the one hand, it could be a burden to the would-be believer. On the other, Mammon, in its place, was stoutly defended. Jesus drove the money-changers from the temple, but advised his disciples to render to Caesar what were his dues. Our clothes are to be given away to those who ask for them. We are to travel lightly, but also to be wise with money, and make the most of our talents.

The economics of the gospels are never straightforward. For example, most of our portrayals of the birth of Jesus can lead to something of a false impression about the place of wealth. Images of clean-swept stables sanitize and romanticize poverty at the nativity: a country-style birth straight from the pages of a Laura Ashley catalogue? The truth is probably more shocking; Jesus was surrounded by animals and filth, with nothing for company save a few rough shepherds. Jesus, it appears, was born poor—a working class lad from Nazareth who made good.

Yet closer attention to the gospels reveals another side to Jesus which is much more comfortable—even middle class? Remember that, traditionally, Jesus was only born in a stable because the hotels were fully booked. The gospels do not imply that Mary and Joseph could not afford lodgings, so they were clearly not that poor. They had their own transport too. Moreover, when the Wise Men came to visit, they brought quite expensive gifts—gold, frankincense and myrrh have never been cheap. Ironically, portraiture of Jesus has hidden his ambivalent class origins to our detriment. We may find, indeed, that the ambivalence that Jesus had towards money, wealth and economics, and found throughout in his teachings, is in fact reflected in his early upbringing.

Indeed, our rather sanitized readings of the birth of Jesus are somewhat wide of the mark, when one begins to explore the Gospels in more depth. Luke's Gospel merely says that there was no room for Mary and Joseph at the place they hoped to stay. But the Greek term translated as 'inn' (*kataluma*) has multiple meanings, among them inn or hostelry—the type used by travellers or pilgrims with their own tents. The word is used only one other time in the New Testament (Luke 22.11 and Mark 14.14) as the place where Jesus observes the Last Supper with the disciples. But it is here that Luke gives us crucial additional information about the *kataluma*: it is a furnished large upper story room within a private house. So the *kataluma* of the last night of Jesus' earthly ministry was the 'upper room'.

Correspondingly, the *kataluma* of Jesus' first night was a basement room in Bethlehem. Mary and Joseph came into town with Mary ready to deliver. They arrived at Joseph's ancestral home, only to find it already full of other family members who had arrived earlier. The exact reason space was not made for a pregnant woman is not known. But it is probably to do with aspects of ritual purity, as well as indicating that the house was already full of more elderly members of Joseph's family, who had priority.

The 'barn' or 'stable' that Mary and Joseph then go to for Jesus to be born is not distant from the *kataluma*. It is almost certainly the cave, basement, or cellar-like structure under the house, which stored the animals at night. Animals are regularly kept in homes at night. By being inside, the animals were protected from the elements and theft. In addition, their presence provided body heat for cool nights, access to milk for the daily meal, and dung as a critical fuel source. In the ancient world, as well as in primitive modern cultures, mangers are also found within the house itself. Many excavations in Palestine have uncovered numerous installations within domestic structures which probably represent ancient mangers. Some are carved, but some are stone-built. Wooden mangers, of course, have not survived the ravages of time, but many 'cribs' of stone have.

There is something of an irony here. Joseph is by trade a *Teknon*, which is the Greek word for craftsmen. Although not of high birth, such people were in great demand for their skills and labour, and it is not inconceivable that Joseph was working on the construction of Herodias' palace at the time of Jesus' birth, and that he himself could have made a rough manger for Jesus. Even for this, Joseph would have needed the money to buy the materials, and would of course have owned his own tools to craft a manger.

So it may actually be quite important that we see Jesus as being, potentially at least, born into a moderately comfortable world. Not rich, certainly, but a household of solid, prudent financial stability. Consider the wider evidence. Mary and Joseph had the money to flee to Egypt and live abroad for a few years in order to escape Herod's wrath. Generally, the poor do not have these resources at their disposal. Carpentry was more of a skilled building industry than a basic utility trade: wood was fundamental to the structure of most housing. The Holy Family could afford a pilgrimage or two. Jesus was educated; well educated, in fact. There were no comprehensive schools in Nazareth, but Jesus had the financial resources to learn reading and writing, and trained as a Rabbi. Even at his death, he owned an expensive seamless robe, and his body was smuggled away by a foreign merchant to be given a 'decent' burial.

Further support for the idea that Jesus knew more about money than meets the eye comes from Eusebius' *Ecclesiastical History*, Book III: 20. The writer, quoting a first-century source, says that the descendants of Jesus family were rounded up during a persecution, with a view to their land being confiscated. Eusebius tells us that 'they had enough to be self-sufficient':[2] not really wealthy, but certainly comfortable.

So if Jesus was from a good, Jewish, middle-class background, what are the implications for Christians? Ironically, they are far more disturbing than if he had been born poor. It would appear that Jesus, in his ministry, turned his back on his class roots, and chose poverty. 'Blessed are poor: for yours is the Kingdom of God' (Luke

6.20, NRSV). Jesus believed a rich man would struggle to gain entry into heaven; he assumed the poor would be there by right.

Jesus made friends amongst the poor—sinners, prostitutes, the mentally ill, widows—and he invariably challenged the wealthy over their pride and complacency. The Christian paradigm, in Jesus at least, is 'sell your possessions . . . take no gold, silver or copper in your belts, no pack for the road . . . ' (Matthew 19.21, 10.9–10), and always bless the beggar, the homeless and the hungry. It is radical stuff, and all rather anti-bourgeois. No wonder Jesus got on people's nerves.

The Shepherds and the Wise Men came bearing gifts for a king. What they found instead was an ordinary family, but in temporary accommodation, struggling with a new baby. It must have been quite a shock. The Wise Men had tried Herod's palace first, but found they got the wrong address. Yet the Gospels record that they still gave their gifts, expensive as they were, and left them at the poor and lowly stable. In their own way, they were quite radical, and they throw a question back to us: what gifts should Christians offer for the homeless, the displaced, the poor and the marginalized? The Christian response to the coming of Jesus must indeed 'cost not less than everything'.[3]

No wonder, then, that the ministry of Jesus was, from the outset, inherently political and economic in character as much as it was 'other-worldly'. This had profound implications for how Christians imagined the new world order. The Gospel of John presents the reader with a Christ who calls Christians out of the world, but at the same time leaves them in it (cf. John 15.19, 17.14, 18.36, etc.). In the same way, the radical words and actions of Jesus on money and wealth appear (at first sight) to point in opposite directions. Yet to only understand Jesus as a radical interferer within the social order of first-century Palestine would be to ignore a core dimension of his agenda: the kingdom of God which is to come. The radical discipleship demanded by Jesus may be said to dwell less on reform and more on revolution. Employment and families are to be forsaken for the kingdom—the ushering in of the new reign of God. Even the dead can be left unburied (cf. Matthew 8.22;

Luke 9.57–62). Moreover, the disciples are not to anticipate reward or rule in this life; all recognition of costly service and devotion is postponed until the end of time and the last judgment, where the wheat will be separated from the chaff, and the righteous rewarded (Matthew 6.19–21).

In very early Christian tradition, the apparent imminence of the kingdom of God led some to give up work, and others to lead a life of celibacy. But by the time the later documents of the New Testament were being written, Christians were being urged to respect and work with temporal authorities, get on with their ordinary labours, live and earn responsibly, and begin to apply gospel principles to this life, rather than speculating on the actual date of the Day of Judgment.

These two distinct traditions within early Christian teaching are closely related. Each act of service (e.g., hospitality, charity, etc.), the extension of costly love (e.g., of turning the other cheek, loving your enemies, etc.), and of vicarious sacrifice points towards the kingdom that is to come. Within Christian tradition, the kingdom is the place where society is reordered; the poor are made rich, captives are liberated, the lame walk and the blind are restored to sight (Luke 4.18–19). It is also the place where impoverished inherit the kingdom, the mourners are comforted, the meek and the peacemakers rewarded, and the persecuted redeemed. (Matthew 5.3–11) In other words, Christian social teaching anticipates the rule of God in prayer and action: 'your kingdom come, your will be done, on earth as it is in heaven.' (Matthew 6.9–13)

This tradition and teaching is reflected in the very first Christian communities. Stephen, the first Christian martyr, is a deacon with special responsibility for the daily distribution of alms to widows and orphans (Acts 6.1–3), reflecting the commitment to charity and service that is advocated in the gospels. In character, the first churches, although diverse in practice and belief, appear nevertheless to have exhibited a shared and radical openness to questions of parity and inclusion. The original spirit of St. Stephen's Day, indeed, is caught in J.M. Neale's famous nineteenth-century carol, celebrating Wenceslas as he tracks down an unknown beggar in a snowstorm to give him a feast. The carol ends with a moral warning:

> Therefore, Christians all, be sure,
> Wealth or rank possessing,
> Ye who now will bless the poor,
> Shall yourselves find blessing.

The early Christian Socialists—men like F.D. Maurice, Stewart Headlam and John Ludlow—understood that God discriminated for the poor, and shared something of the radical nature of Jesus' chosen social incarnation. They worked with Chartists, radicals and other organizations to bring justice for the working class. They argued for universal suffrage, set up colleges and co-operatives, and laboured for the labourer. It was a costly agenda: Maurice lost a Chair in Theology at King's College, London for his trouble. Yet he never lost the imperative: the poor were God's cause, and a truly Christian society would never abandon them.

So what are Christians to be about in a world dominated by market forces and economic issues? The term for 'church' is the simple Greek word *ekklesia*, meaning the 'assembly of the people' who belong to, but are called out of, their community. All over the Mediterranean world, assemblies determined the politics, polity and civic ordering of communities and cities. But they were usually only open to citizens, and the power to speak and vote was normally confined to men. The assemblies of the New Testament church— the deliberate adoption of the more internationalist term must have caused confusion to potential converts, as well as making a point—were, in contrast, inclusive if alternative. In these *ekklesiae*, women were admitted, as were slaves, children, foreigners and other visitors. In other words, the character of the New Testament *ekklesia* represented and embodied a different kind of spiritual and social ordering that eschewed discrimination on grounds of race, gender and other criteria.

Closely allied to the notion of *ekklesia* was the *enclesia*—an idea developed by Coleridge, amongst others,[4] to specify that Christians may not (only) be called out of the world, but are also called into it. Coleridge regarded the idea of *enclesia* as a gospel gospel mandate. Christians were called to be light to the world, the salt of the earth and the leaven in the lump. Correspondingly, churches, for Coleridge, rather than being separatist and alternative bodies within their broader communities, were to be deeply embedded within the civic, economic, social and moral ordering of society, contributing to the overall commonwealth.

Christianity was, from the outset, an inherently political, economically active and profoundly social faith. The expression of Christian faith always challenges the present world order, but is, at the same time, prepared to work within it, regarding nothing as being beyond redemption. It is incarnate, and yet also prophetic. At the same time, Christianity exhibits a typical feature of many world religions. The word 'religion' literally means 'to bind our worship and understanding of God to all of life', and to make a difference to the present in anticipation of God's future. That is why all Christians should welcome the advent of Theonomics. If we are serious about the coming of the kingdom of God, this is the life that we need to engage with and transform, in order to prepare for the next. Theonomics is a most welcome contribution to the agenda for transformation—something that all Christians are committed to.

Martyn Percy
Principal of Ripon College, Cuddesdon

NOTES

1. J Kleist (ed.), 'Epistle to Diognetus', *The Ancient Christian Writers*, no. 6 (New York: Newman Press, 1948), p. 139.
2. Eusebius, *Ecclesiastical History*, Book III, p. 20.
3. The phrase 'cost not less than everything' refers to T. S. Eliot's poem *Little Gidding* (part *V*) in which he describes 'a condition of complete

simplicity (costing not less than everything).' T. S. Eliot, *Four Quartets* (London: Faber & Faber, 1944).

4. Samuel Taylor Coleridge, *On the Constitution of Church and State* (London: Taylor & Hessey, 1839).

CONTENTS

1.   WHAT'S IT ALL ABOUT?

— Andrew Lightbown —

Economics are the method: the object
is to change the heart and soul.
MARGARET THATCHER

Justice is missing because most Americans
do not relate their faith to the economy.
JAMES CUMMINS & WILLIAM OLSON[1]

1.1.   THE ETHICAL DEFICIT

When ENRON, a major American company, collapsed in 2001 shock-waves went around the corporate world. In its heyday, ENRON was held up as a model of how to grow a business, and the rise in the price of its shares was phenomenal, but it was a corporation built on sand, on so-called 'creative accounting' designed to inflate the share price and to cover up the fact that the company was not actually producing anything to back it up. Inevitably, the truth came out: not only did the company fail, wiping out the savings of many investors and leaving the workforce without income, jobs or pensions, its president and chief officers were put on trial and convicted of theft and fraud. So great was the scandal that a play was written about it: *ENRON* by Lucy Prebble. The collapse of ENRON was not an isolated affair: names like Robert Maxwell and Bernard Madoff come to mind. There have also been other scandalous corporate disasters, like the oil spill from the super-tanker Exxon Valdes that devastated the coast of Alaska, poisoning the environment, destroying wildlife, and impoverishing the local community, and in 2010 the fire on BP's oil rig in the Gulf of Mexico with the same consequences. And, of course, we are still living with the economic crisis caused by the near collapse of the banking system in 2008. A play was written about that too: *The Power of Yes*, by David Hare.[2]

None of these were simply unfortunate events: they were all the result of deliberate actions, some clearly illegal, others the result of gross irresponsibility, reckless risk-taking, cutting corners, pushing up the share price, and not being too concerned with doing the right thing, so long as what was done was within the law—just within the letter of the law, that is, rather than the spirit. *The Power of Yes* describes a financial world cut off from reality, where normal considerations of morality, equity, and fairness simply do not apply. David Hare exposes the greed and irresponsibility that were everywhere, but more than this, he describes a world in which cleverness—the ability to dream up complex financial schemes which exploit loopholes in the law—is its own moral justification: because we can do it, we should do it. And because everyone is doing it, it must be right. In a word, the failure was ethical, not financial. From ENRON to the banks to BP what we are looking at is the ethical deficit of modern economic management. There has indeed been a change of soul.

The change of soul we talk about refuses to acknowledge that 'we are all in it together,' that my prosperity is linked to your prosperity, and that some people simply do not possess the material, social, or spiritual resources to make effective and life-affirming choices. Modern economic and political theories seem either to celebrate power, autonomy, and status, leaving individuals to make their own independent choices, or to promote some form of inadequate utilitarian ethic. In both cases minorities and the weak suffer. Economic liberalism and utilitarian philosophy have been two of the most successful evangelistic movements of the last few decades, so successful, in fact, that economic ideas have become a surrogate religion with its own materialist scale of values and understanding of the purpose of life. Economic liberalism suggests that markets somehow, mysteriously, have the potential to sort out all human problems. George Soros, who has accumulated vast personal wealth as a highly sophisticated and skilled market participant, labels this belief 'market fundamentalism.' Soros suggests that market fundamentalism is of no use to the poorest members of our global and local communities.

1.2.   A SPIRITUAL POVERTY

At the same time we have seen the rise of Islam. The violence of the extremists has masked the more basic, underlying demand that economic and social policy, indeed all aspects of public life, should take into account the spiritual dimension of life, which is represented by religious faith. We believe that these events are connected, and point to the fact that not only has economics become divorced from ethics, but that religious faith has much to contribute in re-establishing the connection. For too long, certainly in the West, we have acted as though people only have material needs, and the economic system has operated simply to meet these needs. Paradoxically, we are also only too aware that increasing wealth, increasing the supply of material goods, has not led to greater happiness or well-being. Our economic life as well as our private life needs to take account of the fact that we humans are spiritual and social beings, and that our spiritual needs as well as our material needs should be reflected in the way economics is conceived. This book offers a way of looking at economics from the perspective of faith, and, we believe, offers both a way of saving economics from its limited perspective, and a way forward that will save us from greed, irresponsibility and corruption. It is written from a Christian perspective, but we acknowledge the contribution that others bring from other faith perspectives, for example, Muslim and Buddhist.

The problem we face is at root religious: it is about what we worship, what we place at the centre of our lives. As we have said, economics has become a surrogate religion, and this perhaps is the main reason why it needs to be confronted at the religious level. Christianity, in common with other religions, offers a deeper reality than individual desire and ambition as the focus for our lives, and it provides a scale of values that is based on deeper considerations than material worth; it also takes seriously human weakness and our capacity for wrongdoing, and provides a way of strengthening our inner resources. It is our conviction that the Christian faith offers resources, largely unknown even among Christians, which will help us create the ethical foundation that we need to put our economic house in order.

1.3.   ECONOMY AND THE-OECONOMY

We call this faith perspective 'theonomics', a term designed to convey the idea of theologically inspired, or motivated, economics. Theonomics accepts the basic economic framework of the free market—no one has come up with a better or more efficient framework—but argues that the way we allow the market to operate needs re-configuring. In one way theonomics represents a return to orthodoxy, to the ideas of some of the founding fathers of economics who saw the need to keep economic ideas and institutions connected with other aspects of life, including the spiritual and the moral. Adam Smith, celebrated on the current £20 note, is generally regarded as the founder of modern economic thought. He believed that the foundation of economics was moral philosophy. Not only did he write *The Wealth of Nations*, setting out his view of how the economy worked, but also the *Theory of Moral Sentiments*.[3] The foundational discipline underpinning moral philosophy, even secular moral philosophies, is theology, the branch of knowledge that seeks to understand our spiritual nature and relate human life to the reality of the divine, that is, to something greater than the individual self.

In another way, theonomics is a move away from orthodoxy. Adam Smith saw the economy as a giant machine, a model based on Newtonian physics where the decisions of a myriad of self-seeking individuals combined to create order and harmony, and behind this process he saw a 'divine being', an 'invisible hand', who guided the process so that it replicated the physical world. At the heart of this system was the individual acting rationally in his or her self-interest. One result of this view is that individual preferences inevitably become the basis of moral judgement—if it feels good for you, then it is right for you—and satisfying individual desires becomes the purpose of the economic system. Happiness is believed to come through increasing consumption, thus defining us by our appetites, and the goal of society is to increase material prosperity. By contrast the Christian faith sees the common good as central, and equates love of neighbour with love of self. It insists that the condition of the poorest, rather than the general level of prosperity, is the bottom line in determining the state of the nation. Mohammad Yunus, the founder of Grameen Bank and a Nobel Prize Winner, shares this perspective. He asks why GDP should be measured on the basis of some crude arithmetical average, arguing instead that measuring the rise in income amongst the bottom 20% of the population would provide far greater insights into the real wealth of a particular nation.[4]

Economics seeks to understand the way scarce resources are used and allocated—about how we can use these things economically. Its focus is practical: how to produce goods and services more efficiently, balancing supply and demand, and how prices are determined. It is grafted on to the more basic aspects of life, like social relationships and institutions, ethical and moral values, and beliefs about the purpose and destiny of human life. Economic thinking always requires a guiding philosophy or world view, and economic theories take their validity from these views or philosophies. Economics is a relational practice. Economists who prefer to remove social, political, or faith-based principles from economic life still look to other disciplines to validate their practice. Econometrics, with its preference for mathematical, quantitative and statistical models as guides for economic behaviour, is no different. If economics is, by definition, relational, then it becomes vitally important to ensure that the relationship it enters into with other disciplines is healthy, or, to put it into psychological terms, functional rather than dysfunctional. Just as the human body needs a healthy heart, so does the economy. When we forget that economic action must, by necessity, be guided by some form of ethical orientation the result is frequently calamity. As we have seen, it is misleading to describe the collapse of ENRON and all the other such scandals, including the recent banking crisis, as simply economic disasters; at heart they were ethical failures, and the chilling reality is that they could easily happen again. There is something profoundly wrong at the heart of the Western economic system. From a theonomic perspective, renewing the heart is about pursuing virtue and integrity.

1.4.   VIRTUE

Virtue is the agent of inner change and growth. The pursuit of virtue gives us the capacity to live by higher qualities and standards than those that simply serve our self-interest. We do not hear much about virtue these days; we hear more about values, but the two are not the same. We are encouraged to choose our values, they are part of the way we express our personality (though in fact they generally follow prevailing attitudes), and this is one aspect of the individualist nature of western society. By contrast, virtue accepts that the values and attitudes that make for human flourishing are given, and grow within us through the pursuit of virtue. Alasdair MacIntyre suggests that virtues are public goods;[5] we prefer to think of them as shared and relational assets. Virtue is prior to values: it is about the formation of character, an inner quality or grace that enables us to live a life that is morally good. Virtues need developing through practice, and this means submitting oneself to a guiding set of rules, even when it is inconvenient or painful to do so.

The primary Christian virtue is love, in the sense of self-giving, even to the point of self-sacrifice, and, in economic terms, we suggest this means taking everyone's interests seriously.[6] Two particular virtues, we believe, help us to do this and characterise theonomics, namely humility and reverence. Humility, as we explain in Chapter 2, is widely misunderstood. It is not about doing yourself down, a hand-wringing, self-effacing attitude, but about coming to a proper appreciation of yourself before God and in the community; humility is an inner strength that enables us to give others room to be themselves and to make their contribution to a common endeavour. Reverence is an attitude of the heart that shows deep respect for other people, valuing them as equals. H. Richard Niebuhr put it beautifully when he referred to the reverence that is love, a love that is respectful in its closeness, and which seeks neither to overwhelm, nor be subsumed by, the other. It respects the other's otherness, and does not seek to make him or her into a self-image, nor regard them as a way of self-promotion.[7]

Both humility and reverence point to the difference between individualism and individuality. As Christopher Jamison has said, 'Individualism is simply doing your own thing in your own way and blanking out the other people. Individuality involves bringing your particular contribution to bear on the life of the community, even if that is a difficult contribution for others to accept.'[8]

Virtue gets forgotten in a highly competitive environment, like finance. Paul Moore used to work for HBOS, which was, until recently, one of the major British banks. When Moore became alarmed at the reckless scale of lending he spoke out, and was dismissed. He believes the bank's leaders were not wicked men, but essentially good people who had lost their perspective when it came to business and making money—and for a time, he admitted, that included him too. I know from personal experience that the exclusive focus on making money can lead to a loss of perspective, or rootedness. Focusing on the manufacture of that which is entirely inanimate may lead to a lack of sensitivity to the needs of real people. As St Paul said, 'the love of money is the root of all evil' (1 Timothy 6.10). Money itself is not evil, but our attitudes towards money can lead to an atrophy of the soul.

Ralph Nader, the author of Unsafe at Any Speed, pointed out that, in spite of the competition between them, it did not serve the interests of car manufacturers to make their products any safer.[9] Pursuing your own interests, as Adam Smith believed, does not always take care of other people's interests, nor of the wider public interest. The invisible hand simply cannot be relied on to pursue the common good. Virtue is also marginalised by the emphasis on autonomy, the belief that no other considerations beyond my personal wants are relevant to my welfare. Personal growth and community are irrelevant in a world of autonomous individuals, and the pursuit of virtue becomes pointless.

1.5.   AIMING OFF-TARGET

The enemy of virtue, in Christian understanding, is sin, and we hear even less about sin these days than virtue. The root meaning of sin is an offence against God; we use the term not just to mean wrong devices and desires, but in its more basic Biblical sense of simply missing the mark, being off-target, having the wrong goals, misunderstanding what human life is truly about. Sin is seductive; it works along the grain of our character, using the things that we are good at, that give us a sense of worth, fulfilment, excitement, etc., and pushing us a bit further than we ought to go. So, for example, smart city traders try to become smarter, vying with each other to come up with even more complex derivatives, to pursue even greater returns, and go further than they should. Generally we miss the mark because our starting point is wrong. Virtue begins with what is given, or, more particularly, with what is God-given: 'For everything comes from you, and it is only your gifts that we give to you.' (1 Chronicles 29:14). This describes one of Christianity's core economic beliefs, namely that there is a 'given-ness' about life, especially human nature and the natural order. The acceptance that things, including our own particular gifts and capabilities, are initially given, and therefore involve no special merit on our part, leads to the conclusion that humility is core to theonomic practice. Sin, and especially pride, pushes aside all sense of humility, and frequently leads to catastrophe. This recognition led St. Benedict to stress that community members who used their own distinct gifts with pride and for personal advantage were likely to undermine the stability of the community in which they lived and worked and worshipped.[10]

1.6.   JUSTICE

Another core Christian economic belief is that the economy should serve the needs of justice. At the head of this chapter we placed this quotation: 'Justice is missing because most Americans do not relate their faith to the economy.' (For 'Americans', any of the nations of the developed world, and most of those of the developing world, could be substituted.) This encapsulates one of the world's most pressing problems, the absence of justice or fairness in the distribution of the world's resources. Economically, we are aiming off-target because we have chosen to be blind to the given-ness of life and to injustice, preferring instead to pursue personal wealth and material prosperity. So much so that, as a modern economist, Jane Collier of Cambridge University, has said, economics has come to shape our culture and our view of life:

> The language of economics is the language through which the world is understood, the language by which human and social problems are defined and by which solutions to those problems are expressed. Our lives are dominated by the rituals of 'getting and spending'. Political options

translate into economic decisions; political decisions are
implemented by economic institutions.[11]

This is a reversal of the proper relationship between economics
and ethics, as a result of which we have become hollowed out
as moral beings, and when things go wrong we look to external
controls—laws and regulators like the FSA—to put things right,
rather than our own inner moral resources. In Mere Christianity
C.S. Lewis famously warned against expecting too much from
regulation and legal initiatives; there was little point changing rules
and regulations, he said, if the same people were left in charge,[12]
and, probably, he would not have put much faith in grand macro
policies, believing that they were doomed to failure. Lewis felt
that what really mattered was our hearts. We feel the same. We
have already argued that virtue is important; we also argue that
agency is important. Theologians and economists share two crucial
questions: 'Who do I represent?' and 'Whose interests do I serve?'
The answers to these two questions take us well on the way to
understanding how we, and the institutions we work in or lead,
act in the world.

1.7.   INTEGRITY

Christians, and people of all faiths, cannot escape from the fact that
they live in an economy. In responding to this fact we are faced
essentially with three choices, which we describe as the fatalistic
choice, the parallel choice, and the integrative choice.

The fatalist sighs and asks 'What can I do?' Economic questions
are just too big, too broad and too complex, and so the fatalist
leaves the answers to the big questions in the hands of the experts.
The fatalist hopes that the economists and politicians will 'sort it
out'—a misguided faith in the institution of the ballot box! Fatalism
separates life into secular and sacred spheres, keeping the ethical

and the economic apart. Those seeking the parallel choice also separate life into sacred and secular spheres preferring to live in a holy huddle, turning their backs on social and economic realities. Fundamentalism and isolation are the natural destination of those seeking to live a parallel life, and some Christians take this approach, but it is a dead end. Truer to the mainstream Christian tradition is the remark of Brother Nicholas, a monk of Alton Abbey, who said to me on a recent visit: 'You can't be divorced from economic and social life if you are a Christian. You have to get involved.' Bringing together, integrating the different aspects of our lives is the mark of a mature person; they live with integrity, and we believe that this ought also to be a mark of our economy. Integrity is basic to the Biblical understanding of life. For example, chapters 20 to 23 of Exodus contain a variety of laws covering, among other things, the purchase and emancipation of slaves, criminal offences, civil injuries, duties towards aliens, lending money and agriculture. These laws jostle with others about worship, sacrificial offerings and religious festivals, and no distinction is made between them; they are brought together because they are all equally part of the personal and communal duty to God.

Those who take the path of integrity refuse to live life in separate compartments, and seek to bring together the personal and the political, the ethical and the economic. It is really the only way, and we see it in the work of organizations like Christian Aid, which not only seeks to provide aid to the poor, but also asks why they are poor, and campaigns for structural change in the economic system to remove the causes of poverty. The common good and the pursuit of justice are the inspiration for the integrative choice, as the Lord's Prayer puts it, 'Thy kingdom come, thy will be done in earth as in heaven.' The shape of an integrated ethical economic framework is explored in the next chapter, and it brings together six basic ideas: community, solidarity, justice, gift, service and subsidiarity.

Integration is also about reconciling differences. Rabbi Jonathan Sacks has written about the need to rediscover the ancient religious traditions. In *The Dignity of Difference* he argues that we need to rediscover a sense of solidarity one with another, whilst celebrating the uniqueness of each and every individual.[13] Holding individual needs and the common good in a creative tension characterises the Christian, as well as the Jewish, approach to economic life— it comes from the Old Testament, which both faiths accept as foundational—and it offers a distinct contrast to both of the dominant economic models of the twentieth century, Marxism and capitalism. Both are founded on a misconception of what it means to be human, and Pope John Paul II criticised them for the way in which they exalted the economic over the spiritual:

'[When] the affluent society or the consumer society seeks to defeat Marxism on the level of pure materialism by showing how a free-market society can achieve a greater satisfaction of material needs than communism, while equally excluding spiritual values . . . it agrees with Marxism in the sense that it totally reduces humans to the sphere of economics and the satisfaction of material needs.'[14]

Theonomics seeks the way of integrity, holding individual needs and the common good in a creative tension, and offers a critique both of modern capitalist economic orthodoxy, with its celebration of self-sufficiency, independence and autonomy, and of the Marxist model with its desire to use the individual for statist ends. Theonomics believes in and celebrates interdependence, and has difficulty with the notion that human beings are designed to be either autonomous or self-sufficient; it is deeply relational and integrative.

This book is not a work of either systematic theology or economics. Our objective is much more limited; it is simply to create a space where people of faith, and those who are concerned about the state of the world, who are willing to address the really big questions, can start to think about how they act in the world economically. We take an explicitly bottom-up and institutional perspective for we are interested in what individual, or small groups of people can actually do in the world that they inhabit, irrespective of national or government policy, and the case studies illustrate how various organizations seek to integrate their Christian beliefs with everyday economic activity. Clearly as Christian authors we reject some of the world views that have tended to dominate economic and social life. The Christian perspective maybe counter-cultural, but it leads to a deeper sense of well-being than material prosperity. The organizations and work described in Chapters 7 to 11 are all to some extent counter-cultural, but they are all successful. By focusing on real institutions and real people we hope to provide readers with the confidence and hope that they can make a difference in both the economic and social spheres.

SUMMARY

- Our starting point is the ethical deficit revealed by the banking crisis and other recent corporate failures.
- A major reason for these failures is the way economic ideas have become self-sufficient, cut off from moral and religious perspectives, leading to the view that increasing material prosperity is the way to happiness, and ignoring the spiritual and social dimension of our humanity.
- For some people, in particular the poor, increased material prosperity may be part of an increase in well-being, but it is never the sole factor, and for others, well-being may increase as material assets decrease. Aggregate methods of measuring growth, like GDP, are blunt tools.
- Economics is a secondary discipline, it needs an underlying moral and social philosophy to shape it; thinking and behaving 'theonomically' is about bringing Christian insights to bear on economic activity, re-shaping our economics.
- A particular Christian insight is the need to recover virtue as part of economic management. Virtue is prior to values, the agent of inner change and growth.
- The modern economy is off-target not simply because of the ethical deficit, but also because it sits light to the given-ness of life and the demands of justice. Economic ideas now shape

social policy, despite the fact that social realities are more basic and should shape economic policy.

- The Christian view rejects the division of life into sacred and secular spheres, and seeks to integrate the personal and the political, the ethical and the economic.

- Increased well-being is our chosen metric; it is a function of improved and healthy economic, social and spiritual relationships.

NOTES

1. This quotation from Margaret Thatcher is the concluding sentence to her interview for *The Sunday Times*, 3 May, 1981. The second quotation is from James Cummins and William Olson, *The Whole Truth* (Place of Publication?; Carnegie Melon Classic, 2003).

2. David Hare, *The Power of Yes—A dramatist seeks to understand the financial crisis* (London: Faber & Faber, 2009).

3. Adam Smith, *An Enquiry into the Nature and Causes of the Wealth of Nations* (Chicago: University of Chicago Press, 1977; first published in 1774); Adam Smith, *The Theory of Moral Sentiments* (Cambridge: Cambridge University Press, 2002; first published in 1759).

4. Muhammad Yunus, *Banker to the Poor* (London: Aurum, 2009).

5. Alasdair MacIntyre, *After Virtue* (London: Duckworth, 1981, reprinted 1985).

6. The suggestion that in the business world 'love' means 'taking everyone's interests seriously' originated with Bishop Simon Phipps, Bishop of Lincoln 1974—1987.

7. H Richard Niebuhr is cited in G. Outka, *Agape and Ethical Analysis* (New Haven: Yale University Press, 1972), p. 2.

8. Christopher Jamison OSB, *Finding Sanctuary* (London: Weidenfeld & Nicolson, 2006).

9. Ralph Nader, *Unsafe at Any Speed* (New York: Grossman Publishing, 1965).

10. St Benedict of Nursia was a monk who lived in central Italy between *c.* 480 and 540 AD. His only known writing is the Rule he wrote to govern the life of his monastic community, and the reference here is to Chapter 57. His relevance to theonomics and the content of the Rule are discussed more fully in later chapters.

11. Jane Collier, 'Contemporary Culture and the Role of Economics' in Hugh Montefiore (ed.) *The Gospel and Contemporary Culture* (London: Mowbray, 1992).

12. C.S. Lewis, *Mere Christianity* is based on a series of radio talks that he gave between 1942 and 1944. It was first published in 1952 by Geoffrey Bles.

13. Jonathan Sacks, *The Dignity of Difference* (London: Continuum 2002).Copyright © Jonathan Sacks. Reproduced with permission of Continuum, an imprint of Bloomsbury Publishing Plc.

14. Pope John Paul II is quoted from *Centesimus Annus*, one of the 'social encyclicals' issued by the Roman Catholic Church, and described further in Chapter 2.

2. A CHRISTIAN FRAMEWORK FOR ECONOMICS

— Peter Sills —

Is there not a radical limitation to
economics which renders it inappropriate
to determine social structures?
POPE PAUL VI[1]

2.1. FROM MECHANICS TO ORGANICS

Adam Smith's understanding of the economy as a giant machine guided by an 'invisible hand' was very much a idea of his time, inspired as it was by Newtonian physics, and the invisible hand is more a deist than a Christian conception. Our understanding of both physics and God has moved on since the eighteenth century, but an important part of orthodox economic theory has not. The complexity of the physical world could not give rise to such a mechanistic model today. Since Newton's day we have become aware that fundamental reality is more fluid and more relative. Modern physics teaches us that the fundamental particles of our universe do not have definite properties at all times, and that measurements made in one place affect measurements made in other places.[2] This seems also to describe our everyday experience of economic reality: a world in which nothing is fixed and everything depends on everything else. We also know, from the work of sociologists and psychologists, much more about the complex social and individual motivations that determine economic activity, including personal beliefs and values, but this knowledge has not had sufficient influence on economic theory to change the presuppositions upon which it is founded, although, it must be said, that,not all economists are happy with this, and in the last few years some economists, aware of the inadequacies of mainstream economic theory, have begun to develop a new approach, which they call 'human economics.' A truly human economics needs to take seriously the nature of the market as a social institution, the injustice of 'free market' outcomes, and the actual motivations and values that determine economic behaviour. Economists need to develop an organic model in place of the Smithian mechanical model, and this chapter sketches out a Christian basis for such a model.

There have been markets as long as there have been people, and while it is true that no better institution has been found to manage the processes of production, distribution and exchange, it is also true that market mechanisms, like those of any social institution, operate in the interests of those best placed to operate them, namely those who come to the market with the most resources—an organic reality to which the invisible hand is blind. As Pope Pius XI put it, writing after the Wall Street crash of 1929, 'immense power and despotic economic domination' are concentrated in the hands of a few, 'limitless free competition permits the survival of those only who are the strongest, and this often means those who fight most relentlessly, [and] who pay least heed to the dictates of conscience.' (Pius XI, *Quadragesimo Anno,* 1931) Adam Smith's mechanical view of the economy focussed on its processes with only a limited interest in its outcomes, namely productive outcomes,,how to produce more at lower cost, rather than social outcomes, the way wealth, goods and services are distributed. At the same time, he lived in an age in which Christian moral values still shaped western society and provided an ethical framework for economic activity, and this, to some extent, compensated for the blindness of the invisible hand. It was, however, a moral world in which social injustices were accepted as part of the natural order: 'the rich man in his castle, the poor man at his gate.'[3] Just as our understanding of physics and divinity has moved on since the eighteenth century, so also have our notions of social justice and responsibility. Economic injustice is no longer accepted as part of the natural order, and poverty is now acknowledged to be a major cause of ill-health, social dysfunction and poor productivity.

Our expectations of the economic system have also changed. Christian thinkers and activists were instrumental in the late-nineteenth and twentieth centuries in bringing about this change, and have continued to work for a more humane economics as witnessed in their leadership of 'Jubilee 2000', the campaign to remit the unpayable debts of the world's poorest nations. This campaign tapped into a widespread moral concern that went well beyond the Church. It was part of the outrage at the growing gulf between ethics and politics that characterised the closing decades of the twentieth century, and which contributed to the atrophy of personal moral responsibility that brought about the collapse of ENRON and the near-collapse of the banks in 2008. This moral atrophy was part of a general rejection of given moral values, one of the results of the economic individualism of Adam Smith, and more particularly of the application of his ideas by his more radical disciples in the 1980s. But outrage at the moral failings of others is not enough to bring about the change of heart necessary to transform the economic system; we believe that transforming the old economic order into a new one adequate for our age requires a different supporting philosophy for economic life, and that philosophy needs to be based on Christian insights.

2.2.   A NEW FRAMEWORK

'Bringing Christian insights to bear on the ongoing issues in the modern world, not least in the economic order, is not easy,' said Ronald Preston in 1991, and his caution arose in part from the difficulty of using the Bible as a source of social ethics.[4] The Biblical world is so far removed from our own that it is not possible simply to move from the one to the other, but basic human needs, aspirations and temptations remain much the same from age to age, and so therefore do the ethical tensions of everyday life. While the Biblical rules are remote from our situation, the values that underlie them have a very contemporary relevance. Accordingly, most of those who have sought to make connections between Biblical principles and modern life, including Ronald Preston, do so in two stages: first they identify the basic moral values inherent in the text, and then they ask what those values might mean when applied to contemporary life. For example, understanding the world as something created, rather than the result of the interplay of chance and necessity, gives it a particular character, like that of a work of art. Appropriate responses are reverence and respect rather than exploitation and abuse, and from this flow practical policies for conservation and responsible use. The pressure on non-replaceable natural resources brought about by exploitation legitimised by modern economics has brought us to the same point, but the ethical approach gets us there more directly and with more time to take appropriate action when things go wrong. Our theonomic approach is much the same, and we suggest six values that provide the foundation for an organic economic model: Community, Justice, Gift, Solidarity, Service and Subsidiarity. These values are drawn from the Bible and Christian social teaching. Modern Christian social thought began to develop in the nineteenth century in the face of the social evils described, for example, in the novels of Charles Dickens, and caused by the unrestrained application of *laissez-faire* ideas. There is a notable consensus between the different Churches on social issues; the most developed body of teaching is that of the so-called 'Social Encyclicals' issued by the Roman Catholic Church, and this will be used to illustrate the general approach.

2.2.1.   COMMUNITY

Community is a term widely used today to indicate any kind of collective body, from 'the international community' to 'the cycling community', so much so that it has been evacuated of meaning. In Biblical terms it indicates a community of memory, whose bonds come from a shared story and shared values, binding them together at a deeper level than the material and the protection of common interests. The Hebrew understanding of the relation between the individual and society was markedly different to that of other ancient cultures, as T W Manson explains. In Athens, he said, a man would be proud of his cultural and political heritage, and property, rights and privileges would be jealously guarded. 'The Israelite's attitude to Israel was different. The outstanding feature in it is the intense awareness of corporate solidarity. The members of a clan or tribe in Israel feel themselves as parts of a single living whole.'[5] Compared to Roman law, Hebrew law was much less concerned with rights of property and much more concerned with rights of personality. The basic unit of society was not so much the person as 'the person-in-community', and the primary criterion for economic activity was the well-being of the community. The communal interest takes precedence over the individual interest, but not in a way that de-humanises the individual. Thus the Biblical model is differentiated from both laissez-faire and totalitarian economic models. The primacy of the communal interest is expressed typically in a solidarity between the classes with a duty of generosity towards the poor being accepted by the rich, thus ameliorating the inequalities of economic power. Laissez-faire capitalism works in the opposite direction, and the resulting social divisions prompted Pope Leo XIII to issue the first of the social encyclicals, *Rerum Novarum*, in 1891; the language pulls no punches, it is both forceful and striking:

> . . . it has come to pass that working-men have been surrendered, isolated and helpless, to the hard-heartedness of employers and the greed of unchecked competition. The

mischief has been increased by rapacious usury, which, although more than once condemned by the Church, is nevertheless, under a different guise, with the like injustice, still practised by covetous and grasping men. To this must be added that the hiring of labour and the conduct of trade are concentrated in the hands of comparatively few; so that a small number of very rich men have been able to lay upon the teeming masses of the labouring poor a yoke little better than that of slavery itself.

Pope Leo's social concern is an expression of the divine concern for the poor rather than a political manifesto, and he was equally critical of socialism, particularly its advocacy of common ownership which he saw as destroying the natural right of property. Later in the letter he develops the idea of the 'common good' as a positive duty 'to make sure that the laws and institutions, the general character and administration of the commonwealth shall be such as to produce of themselves public well-being and private prosperity.' The concept of the common good was developed by Pope John XXIII in *Mater et Magistra* (1961). It brings together the social and economic interests of the community; it is about taking everyone's interests seriously, and, in practical terms, it requires as near full employment as possible, a balance between wages and prices, ensuring the accessibility of social goods and services, reducing social and economic inequalities, and taking steps to ensure that future generations are not impoverished by the actions of the present generation. Maintaining the provision of communal goods and services without which society cannot function is a basic duty of the state, and the common good requires a balance to be struck between social efficiency and economic efficiency, so, for example, social efficiency requires a national postal service at uniform prices across the country, although differential prices would be economically more efficient.

Community also has its application to corporate life. While profits are a legitimate aim of a business, being an indication that it is functioning efficiently, from a Christian perspective profits are not the sole aim, nor indeed are they the 'bottom line':

> The purpose of a business firm is not simply to make a profit, but is to be found in its very existence as a community of persons who in various ways are endeavouring to satisfy their basic needs, and who form a particular group at the service of the whole of society. Profit is a regulator of the life of a business, but it is not the only one; other human and moral factors must also be considered which, in the long term, are at least equally important for the life of a business.
>
> *John Paul II, Centesimus Annus*

2.2.2. SOLIDARITY

In the Biblical view, taking the person-in-community as the unit for decision-making places a high value on generosity towards the poor; indeed, one of the consistent themes of both the Old and New Testaments is the divine concern for the poor, the widow, the orphan, and the stranger—in other words, those easily overlooked in a prosperous society because of their lack of economic power. So it is written:

> When you reap the harvest in your land, do not reap right up to the edges of your field, or gather the gleanings of your crop . Do not completely strip your vineyard, or pick up the fallen grapes; leave them for the poor and for the alien.
>
> *Leviticus 19.9–10*

It follows that, from a Christian perspective, it is the condition of the poor rather than the general level of prosperity that determines the state of a society, and this clearly has implications for the use of common economic measures like GDP. The lack of solidarity today is seen in the massive (and growing) gap between the rich and the less well-off. Pay differentials, particularly in banking, have lost contact with both social reality and personal need, and they undermine social cohesion. There is something profoundly disordered about a society in which some can earn in a year hundreds of times more than most will earn in a lifetime. Today we are defined as consumers, and our consumer goods are a measure of our worth; against this, Christians define us by our humanity, by our capacity for love and relationships, and believe that private property is not unconditional right:

> No one is justified in keeping for his exclusive use whatever he does not need when others lack necessities ... [T]he right to property must never be exercised to the detriment of the common good.
>
> ### Paul VI, Populorum Progressio, 1967

These principles are reflected in Jesus' teaching, especially the dignity of each individual person, whether rich or poor, and the concern for the good of the neighbour, a concept that he widened significantly, crossing racial, religious and social groups, to include anyone in need, as, for example, in the Parable of the Good Samaritan (Luke 10.25–37). It is significant that Matthew ends his account of Jesus' teaching on this note. In the parable of the Last Judgement, those who enter the Kingdom are those who have aided those in need, namely the hungry, the thirsty, the strangers, the naked, the sick, and the prisoners (Matthew 25.31–46). It teaches more than the importance of private charity: to care for those in dire need is not simply to reflect God's 'preferential option for the poor', it is to act on the basis that salvation is communal; an individual's eternal destiny cannot be separated from that of his neighbour.

Solidarity, while egalitarian in nature, does not issue in a doctrine of strict equality; riches are not condemned per se, and differences in wealth are tolerated in the Biblical picture of human society, but, nevertheless, they are subject to the demands of that solidarity. Riches bring with them an obligation to help the poor, and the tendency over time to accommodate the Biblical demands to those considered prudent in a more advanced commercial society has to be resisted.

2.2.3.   JUSTICE

Equality in the Bible is the basic equality of every person in the sight of God; beyond that, how people are treated is seen as a matter of justice, rather than equality. Justice requires respect for the particular needs of each person; thus Christian equality is not a crude measure—everyone getting the same, but a just measure— each receiving according to need. Economic activity is not a law unto itself. As we have seen, trade and craft are no different from praise and sacrifice; all are carried out under God and are subject equally to his laws. Economic activity is not exempted from the divine demands of justice and fairness, and thus a purely utilitarian approach to ethics, as favoured by economic theory, is, from the Biblical perspective, inadequate.

In today's terms the Biblical view of justice means *distributive* justice and not simply *procedural* justice, and Christian social teaching has developed what it terms the 'preferential option for the poor'. Paul VI explained it thus: 'In teaching us charity, the Gospel instructs us in the preferential respect due to the poor and the special situation they have in society: the more fortunate should renounce some of their rights so as to place their goods more generously at the service of others.' Paul VI is at pains to set the preferential option within the context of a mutual solidarity in which the poor also have their duty to the common good: 'If, beyond legal rules, there is really no deeper feeling of respect for and service to others, then even equality before the law can serve as an alibi for flagrant discrimination, continued exploitation and actual contempt. Without a renewed education in solidarity, an over-emphasis of equality can give rise to an individualism in which each one claims his own rights without wishing to be answerable for the common good.' (Paul VI, *Octagesima Adveniens*) The Christian idea of justice also includes restoration and reconciliation, which give it a deeper and more profound character than secular theories. Restoration and reconciliation require self-sacrifice and humility, and our model of this approach to life is that of Jesus of Nazareth. A theonomic approach reflects this priority, and examples of restorative and affirmative action in favour of the poor are given in later chapters.

Where justice does require equal treatment is in fair and honest dealing, and this is a marked feature of both the Law and the Prophets. For example, we read in Leviticus:

You are not to pervert justice, either by favouring the poor or by subservience to the great. You are to administer justice to your fellow-countryman with strict fairness ... You are not to falsify measures of length, weight, or quantity. You must use true scales and weights, true dry and liquid measures.. (Leviticus 19.15, 19.35–36)

In the same vein the prophet Isaiah urged the people to 'Pursue justice, guide the oppressed; uphold the rights of the fatherless, and plead the widow's cause.' (Isaiah 1.17). He denounced moneylenders for their greed, the elders for grinding the faces of the poor, and legislators for the injustice of their laws. It all has a striking contemporary resonance!

2.2.4.   GIFT

The land occupied a special place in ancient Israel: it was seen as a gift and not a right, and outside the category of normally tradeable commodities. Today, although Christian social thought has not taken over this view, the given-ness of Creation is affirmed in the insistence that the earth was given for the use and enjoyment of all, and a basic limit is placed on the market: there are some things which lie outside the category of tradeable commodities, like gifts, and some needs which cannot be satisfied by market mechanisms. 'There are collective and qualitative needs which cannot be satisfied by market mechanisms. There are important human needs which escape its logic. There are goods which by their very nature cannot and must not be bought or sold.' (John-Paul II, *Centesimus Annus*)

The principle of gift places limits on rights of ownership, and although private property is basic to individual worth and well-being, it is subordinate to common use, and proper care for the environment places constraints on the way it is used. The special rules in ancient Israel concerning the land, e.g. that it could not be sold outright, were designed to prevent the permanent impoverishment of the poor—in line with the ancient prohibition against the permanent human domination of persons and property. In a later age Jesus said that 'where someone has been given much, much will be expected of him; and the more he has had entrusted to him the more will be demanded of him.' (Luke 12.48), Ownership brings responsibilities as well as freedom, and Jesus' remark was made in the context of possessions, owners and stewards; personal security increases the personal duty of caring. The law of Israel, with its concern for the poor and the stranger, reverses the assumption of a coercive society that possession and power enable one to sit light to the law. Caring for those without possessions is one of the basic obligations of the propertied class.

Land also has a symbolic value, standing for the whole of Creation, which is to be seen as the work and gift of God with its own inherent goodness. It is given to meet the needs of all creatures, and our duty towards it is to use it and to care for it responsibly; in other words, to be good stewards. Stewardship requires an ecological perspective, and points to the excessive and disordered way in which humanity consumes the resources of the earth, an attitude based on an anthropological error: human cleverness blinds us to the truth that Creation is God's gift.

> Man thinks that he can make arbitrary use of the earth, subjecting it without restraint to his will, as though it did not have its own requisites and a prior God-given purpose, which man can indeed develop but must not betray. Instead of carrying out his role as a co-operator with God in the work of creation, man sets himself up in place of God and

> thus ends up provoking a rebellion on the part of nature,
> which is more tyrannised than governed by him.
>
> *John-Paul II, Centesimus Annus*

2.2.5.   SERVICE

Community, solidarity, justice and gift shape the way political power and economic leadership are exercised, and the Biblical model is service rather than dominion. In Christian understanding, to lead is to serve. Jesus contrasted the way of the world, where 'kings lord it over their subjects; and those in authority are given the title Benefactor,' with his own way: 'Not so with you: on the contrary, the greatest among you must bear himself like the youngest, the one who rules like the one who serves.' (Luke 22.25–26) To serve is to place the needs of others above your own, and to have regard for the common good; it reflects the limitations placed on property and ownership, and seeks to advance the demands of justice. It is easier for those who serve to understand the social and not just the economic nature of work, and that good work should help, not hinder, the worker's personal and moral development. Not surprisingly, in the Christian understanding, work has a moral nature, and labour takes priority over capital—not in a Marxist sense, but simply because people are more important than systems. It is wrong to treat labour solely on the basis of its economic function; people are more than economic units, a truth that the term 'human resources' does not quite reflect.

How does the principle of service bear on incentives? Like his contemporaries, Jesus took the reward principle for granted, as, for instance, in his teaching about the heavenly rewards awaiting those who avoided ostentation in alms-giving and prayer (Matthew 6.1–18), but it is clear that he understood 'reward' in a spiritual way, coming more from the grace of God than from human merit. The essential characteristic of the Christian ethic is that it is a response ethic, an ethic of gratitude. The life of joyous obedience is the normal, spontaneous response to the gifts of God. Time and again we are reminded that our worth is God-given, it does not depend on how much we earn, the power we exercise, the possessions we acquire; our reward is to know that we have used our gifts and abilities to serve humanity and to conserve the natural world. Somehow we need to find a way back to a culture of reasonable monetary rewards in place of the excessive salaries and bonuses that the free market legitimises. We hear a lot about the service economy these days; a theo-economy is an economy built on service.

2.3.   SUBSIDIARITY

Subsidiarity is necessary for community, limiting the power of the state to those matters that cannot be dealt with by lower, more immediate levels of social organization. Just as we understand God to have shared with men and women the responsibility for Creation and one another, so the exercise of earthly power is to be a shared venture. Although subsidiarity has become a principle of political life, particularly in the European Union, its religious origins are not acknowledged. It seeks to keep decisions and responsibility at a human level, and is particularly important in a complex age when people feel powerless and demoralised. Although in modern times much that was formerly done by small groups can now only be done by large associations, nonetheless 'just as it is wrong to withdraw from the individual and commit to a group what private enterprise and industry can accomplish, so too it is an injustice, a grave evil and a disturbance of right order, for a larger and higher association to arrogate to itself functions which can be performed efficiently by smaller and lower societies . . . Of its very nature the true aim of all social activity should be to help members of the social body, but never to destroy or absorb them.' (Pius XI, *Quadragesimo Anno*) In the Christian view, first place in economic affairs should be given to individual, private initiative, and the 'precautionary activities of public authorities in the economic field, although widespread and penetrating, should be such that they not only avoid restricting the freedom of private citizens, but also increase it . . . This implies that whatever be the economic system, it allow and facilitate for every individual the opportunity to engage in productive activity.' (John XXIII, *Mater et Magistra*)

SUMMARY

The Christian view sees economic freedom as one element of human freedom, and when it becomes autonomous it looses its necessary relationship with the human person and ends up as a source of alienation and oppression. Given the organic nature of human society, economic structures need to evolve continually, and keep in touch with the more basic social structures. Central to the Christian view is the conviction that the economic order must be subordinated to the moral order; the decision to invest in one place rather than another are moral and cultural choices, whatever the overt basis on which they are made, and ownership of the means of production becomes illegitimate when it seeks profits at the expense of the overall expansion of work and the wealth of society. The collapse of communism left free-market capitalism as the only economic model, and it is tempting to assume that its values and way of operating are the only available option in other words, that there is no alternative. Perhaps, in structural terms, that is correct, but, in terms of values, it is not, and our theonomic approach seeks to contain the operations of the market within a set of values that reflect our spiritual as well as our material needs.

'What is being proposed as an alternative is not the socialist system, which in fact turns out to be state capitalism, but rather a society of free work, of enterprise and of participation. Such a society is not directed against the market, but demands that the market be appropriately controlled by the forces of society and by the state, so as to guarantee that the basic needs of the whole of society are satisfied.' (John Paul II, *Centesimus Annus*).

2.4.   FROM HEAD TO HEART

It is all very well sketching out this framework, but how do we get it to work? There is of course a role for the law. Setting the legal framework for economic activity is accepted as one of the basic functions of government, and indeed all governments constantly amend the relevant laws as political philosophies change and new needs arise. For example, a major cause of the near collapse of the banks in 2008 is generally seen to have been the abolition some years previously of the institutional division between investment and retail banking, which allowed the toxic risks of investment banking to spill over and poison the retail arm. Laws, of course, are the outworking of political policy and preference, and the framework described in the last section sets out some clear goals and preferences that should be set by legislation. For example, requiring companies to act in the interests of their employees, customers and other stakeholders, and not just in the interests of the shareholders, would reflect better the Christian understanding of the business firm as a community; likewise, requiring tax to be paid on profits in the country where they are earned, and not where the company is registered, would reflect the principle of solidarity. But an inadequate legal framework was not the only cause of the banking crisis: an equally large part was the attitude of the bankers, and of the regulators (part of the ENRON scandal was the failure of the accounting firm Arthur Anderson to audit the accounts properly; that firm also collapsed). Laws can only do so much, they have to be interpreted and applied, and the law depends on the attitude of the person applying it if it is to have its intended effect. In the corporate world, and especially the financial world, many people are employed to find ways around the law; the schemes they invent may comply with the letter of the law, but defy its spirit. Something more than an appropriate legal framework is needed in a theo-economy, and that is the pursuit of virtue.

As we noted in Chapter 1, virtue is an inner strength or grace that enables us to live a life that is morally good. It is a natural capacity, like language, love, or prayer, which everyone is born with, but which needs to be developed if it is to shape our lives. In classical philosophy there are four cardinal virtues: prudence, justice, temperance and fortitude.

- **Prudence** is the ability to discern what is both necessary and possible. Prudence is practical wisdom, the ability to see clearly and choose a course of action that will achieve its aims, rather than one which is ideal but likely to fail.
- **Temperance** is the capacity to restrain oneself in provocation and desire. Temperance is being sufficiently self-controlled to be able to moderate one's appetites and not be dominated by other people.
- **Fortitude** is moral strength or courage, particularly in enduring pain and adversity. Fortitude also helps us to withstand temptation and being misunderstood.
- **Justice** is doing the right thing according to morality, equity, law, and reason. Justice ensures that decisions are well-founded, and treats everyone fairly as an individual.

In a public discussion in 2010 Rowan Williams, then Archbishop of Canterbury, called for these virtues to be incorporated into the economic system.[6] Indeed, they ought to be as there is something in each of these qualities about seeing the wider picture, and being prepared to go beyond one's personal interests; but there are powerful factors at work today that limit our frame of reference, and inhibit the pursuit of virtue, and among them are two of the leitmotifs of the modern western world, competition and autonomy, to which we also referred in Chapter 1. However, understanding what virtue is and becoming virtuous are rather different things. Allowing virtue to shape our lives so that, for example, it affects the way we decide to invest money, the way we treat our staff, customers and business associates, the way we compete with others, and determine the obligations we accept towards the wider society requires a journey of personal formation (how many programmes for professional development include growth in virtue?). Many in the Church and in the business world are finding help in the pursuit of virtue in an unlikely place: the teaching of a fifth-century monk, St Benedict of Nursia.[7]

Benedict lived in another time of great social change as the Roman Empire decayed and was replaced by barbarian rule—indeed, many have seen parallels with our own times! Repelled by the worldliness and corruption of ancient Rome, he sought a new direction in solitude. His holiness attracted others, and in time he formed them into a community of monks, and wrote a Rule to order their common life. It sets out the personal qualities and basic institutional structure necessary for those who wish to live and work together to achieve a common goal. The wisdom of the Rule still speaks across the centuries, offering to all, whether religious or not, a balanced way of life that values community and solidarity, seeks justice and integrity, and nurtures personal growth in virtue. The basic Benedictine virtue is humility. Humility is generally thought of in negative terms: self-effacing, doing yourself down, having a poor self image, but that is not what it is really about. The word 'humility' comes from the Latin humus, meaning 'earth'. Humility is about being earthed, being in touch with what is real, with the source of our being. Humility is not a weakness but a strength, an inner strength that comes from a true appreciation of our place in the world—in Christian terms, before God—and within the community; a strength that means that you do not have to have your own way all the time. As Christopher Jamison, a modern-day Benedictine abbot, has said, 'Humility helps us to achieve an inner freedom that frees us from selfish impulses and allows us to be shaped by other people's lives.'[8] Humility is an essential foundation for the cardinal virtues; it is like a narrow door that we have to enter in order to find the treasure within—our true selves—and with it come attitudes that are capable of transforming our economic life. Humility enables the more effective formation of community, and the pursuit of justice and solidarity; it stops us from seeking excessive rewards, placing the emphasis more on personal fulfilment and job-satisfaction.

In the Sermon on the Mount, Jesus re-stated important aspects of the Israelite laws, placing the emphasis on the spirit rather than the letter, for example: 'You have heard that our forefathers were told "Do not commit murder; anyone who commits murder must be brought to justice." But what I tell you is this: Anyone who nurses anger against his brother must be brought to justice.' (Matthew 5.21–22) Obeying the 'higher law' is only possible for those who have grown in virtue. In the same vein Jesus said, 'Do not store up for yourselves treasure on earth, where moth and rust destroy, and thieves break in and steal; but store up treasure in heaven, where neither moth nor rust will destroy, nor thieves break in and steal. For where your heart is, there will your treasure be also. (Matthew 6.19–21) Virtue is that treasure in heaven; a theo-economy is an economy shaped by virtuous leaders and directed to the common good.

SUMMARY

- Economic theory is based on an outmoded mechanical model where the focus is on processes and productivity, not on just outcomes.
- Social injustice is no longer accepted as part of the natural order; a new organic economic model is required, and this needs a new supporting philosophy which Christian insights can provide.
- This theonomic model is based on six principles: Community, Solidarity, Justice, Gift, Service and Subsidiarity.
- While law has an important part to play in providing the economic structure, it is not enough; a new spirit is also required.
- This new spirit is to be found through the pursuit of virtue, an inner spiritual strength or grace that enables us to live a life that is morally good, and this requires the discipline of an inner journey.
- The four classical virtues of Prudence, Temperance, Fortitude

and Justice need to be recovered in economic life.

▪ Humility, being earthed, in touch with what is real, is the path to growth in virtue and the foundation for the classical virtues.

NOTES

1. The chapter head quotation is from *Octagesimo Adveniens*, one of the 'social encyclicals'. The encyclical letters cited in this book are published by Libreria Editrice Vaticana (copyright © Libreria Editrice Vaticana); they all have Latin titles based on their opening words. *Rerum novarum* means 'a new thing', and refers to the new social and economic situation brought about by the spread of democracy and *laissez-faire* capitalism, and the rise of communism. The other social encyclicals were mostly written to mark anniversaries of *Rerum Novarum*: *Quadragesimo Anno* marked the fortieth anniversary in 1931, *Mater et Magistra* the sixtieth in 1961, *Octagesimo Adveniens* the eightieth in 1971, and *Centesimus Aunnus* the centenary in 1991.

2. See further Chad Orzel, How to Teach Quantum Physics to Your Dog (Oxford: One World Publications, 2010)

3. The line about the rich man in his castle and the poor man at his gate comes from the well-know Victorian hymn 'All things bright and beautiful', written by Mrs C F Alexander, and published in 1848. Most modern hymnals omit the relevant verse: 'The rich man in his castle, / The poor man at his gate, / He made them, high or lowly, / And ordered their estate'. This Victorian view of the divine order is incompatible with the modern understanding of both the nature of God and of social order.

4. The quotation from Ronald Preston is from *Religion and the Ambiguities of Capitalism* (London: SCM Press, 1991), p.107.

5. T.W. Manson, *Ethics and the Gospel* (London: SCM Press, 1960), p. 168.

6. The public discussion referred to was between Archbishop Rowan Williams, the psychoanalyst Susie Orbach, and the sociologist Richard Sennet; it is reported in 'Beyond Capitalism' by Christopher Lamb

(*The Tablet*, 4th April 2009). Reproduced with permission of the publisher of The Tablet (http://www.thetablet.co.uk).

7. St Benedict of Nursia lived *circa* AD 480—540. Little is known about him apart from the Rule that he wrote, but it is likely that he came from a well-to-do family because as a young man he was sent to study in Rome. The decadence and immorality of Roman life repelled him, and he moved to Subiaco, where, after living for some years as a hermit, he accepted the invitation of some local monks to become their abbot. All did not go well, and he moved to Monte Cassino, where he wrote a Rule to govern the life of his monks, and this was the beginning of the Benedictine Order, which remains one of the main monastic orders of the Church. Benedict's teaching is contained in the Rule; no other writing of his survives. After Benedict's death Pope Gregory the Great wrote a hagiography, *The Life and Miracles of St Benedict*. The Life and the Rule are both published by the Liturgical Press, Collegeville, Minnesota.

8. Abbot Christopher Jamison OSB is quoted from the BBC series *The Monastery* (2005)

3.　A FRAMEWORK FOR FLOURISHING

— Alan Hargrave —

*The novice should be clearly told all the
hardships and difficulties which will lead him
to God . . . When he is to be received he is to
come before the whole community and promise:
stability, conversion of life and obedience.*

ST BENEDICT OF NURSIA[1]

A couple of years ago I was invited to preach at evensong at St John's College, Cambridge. I occasionally get invited to preach at Cambridge colleges and I never feel very comfortable about it. Evensong can be a bit of an ordeal. There are a lot of unwritten rules which are easy to get wrong. What to wear? Where to put yourself in the procession? Where to sit? When to stand up? Which book to use—and what page? Where to preach from—and when—and how long for? I think of all the famous and exceedingly clever people who have preached here—or who are sitting in the chapel right now—and it is pretty intimidating. So, no point trying to compete—just be yourself and try to look calm! Luckily, they do not ask the preacher to process—they have obviously lost a few preachers in previous processions, so it's deemed better to put them safely in their stall beforehand. Luckily it all goes off reasonably smoothly, despite me having preached for far too long. Then drinks with the choir, none of whom really want to get landed with the preacher.

But its not just the preaching. Its the 'High Table' supper afterwards, and all the unfamiliar customs and rituals that go with it. You never know who you will be sitting next to. I remember dining at one of the other colleges. I was sitting next to an elderly man who was dribbling soup down his shirt. The chaplain said: 'Ah Alan, let me introduce you to Lord 'Smith', former Master of the College and Nobel Prize winner in Chemistry.' So you have to watch your Ps and Qs—not something I am good at. Luckily they don't ask me to say grace, which is in Latin, not a language I am overly familiar with. After a rather esoteric discussion with one of the fellows over dinner on the subject of whether or not the students should have the same menu as we are enjoying at High Table, we finish the meal and are invited retire to the 'fire circle'. What on earth can that be? It sounds like a Masonic ritual.

However, it turns out to be a semi-circle of chairs arranged around a roaring fire in the Senior Common Room. A white gloved waiter brings us glasses of port and madeira, and we continue in polite conversation until the waiter returns with a silver tray. On it stand two tiny silver boxes. He offers them to me. This is it! The trap I have been dreading. What am I supposed to do? Are they a gift for preaching? Should I choose one and put it in my pocket? What if I pick up the wrong one? Perhaps I should say a prayer of blessing over them? The Dean can clearly see my anxious expression. He leans over and whispers, 'It's snuff. Would you care to take some?' I decline the offer. Soon people start to leave, which gives me my excuse. I dash off into the gloom, back into the comfortingly familiar world of loud, drunken teenagers walking the streets at night.

And yet, despite this quaint, anachronistic existence, which has more in common with the fifteenth than the twenty-first century, I have to remind myself that St John's College is a place at the cutting edge of creativity, brilliance, invention and advancement in almost every discipline you care to think of. Perhaps part of the reason 'why' is because of, not despite, those ancient practices; tradition, continuity, security—what you might call stability—and rules—written and unwritten—that you need to obey if you are to be admitted and continue in that hallowed institution. And also a commitment to transformation, being at the cutting edge of innovative thought and action, striving for excellence and pushing back the frontiers in arts, humanities and science.

Those ancient Cambridge colleges were, of course, modelled on monastic communities, which in turn often followed the Rule of Saint Benedict, mentioned in the last chapter. The Rule is full of wisdom, compassion and balance, so much so that it has been a best seller ever since. Indeed, as Peter Sills said, there is growing interest, even in the business world, in exploring how Benedict's Rule can help us in our economic life today. Benedictine communities are based around three vows, which the monks take at their profession. These are not the vows of poverty, chastity and obedience, which we often associate with religious life. Benedictine vows are to Obedience, Stability and *Conversatio Morum*, which is not easy to translate, but means something like: 'sticking with the Rule of the monastery in order that we and others might be transformed into the likeness of Christ'.[2] They offer, I believe, a 'Framework for Flourishing', not just for religious communities or Cambridge colleges, but for wider society and for our economic life as well. So, let us consider these three vows, in terms both of our individual lives, and in terms the businesses, organizations, and communities we are each involved with in the wider world.

3.1.   OBEDIENCE

Each of the three vows has its downside. It is capable of abuse. Try telling people in Libya who have suffered under Gaddafi, or women who have suffered years of abuse from men, that they should be obedient! I was talking one day about obedience with a friend, who for many years was a Roman Catholic nun, before finally leaving her order. She listened for a while and then said: 'Obedience is what I'm in permanent recovery from.' It can be abused, and it sadly often is, even in places like St John's College. It can be a way of putting people down, keeping them in their place, unhelpfully exerting power, promoting elitism.

But, in fact, Benedict's Rule recognises this danger and makes provision to avoid such abuse. Esther de Waal, who has written in depth about the Rule, says that the Latin word for obedience, *oboedire*, means 'to listen to'.[3] Benedict's Rule itself begins with that thought: 'Listen carefully my son to the instruction of your master. Turn the ear of your heart to the advice of a loving father. Welcome it, and put it into practice.' (*RSB*, Prologue 1) What is being talked about here is paying such close attention that what we hear becomes part of us, enters deep within us, begins to form us and to determine our attitudes and actions. This is not so much about obeying rules as developing values—virtues—which become embedded within us and which naturally inform and direct our attitudes and our actions. People in business talk about a particular 'culture' in a company or a department. Such cultures are not ethically neutral. What Benedict is seeking to achieve by 'Obedience' is to set out and follow principles which promote human flourishing at its deepest level. And such flourishing is not anti-business, since for centuries monasteries were at the centre of the economic activities of the communities in which they were situated.

Along with Obedience comes accountability. To whom are we answerable? What are the consequences if we fail to comply with the rules? In a monastery that is clear: accountability is to the Abbot, and he decides the sanctions for falling short. It is probably reasonably clear at the places where most of us work. However, the development of a culture in which we are only, in the end, accountable to shareholders has undermined the importance of business to the wider community and along with it the concept of 'stewardship' of what we have been entrusted with. Not only that, but loosening the 'Rules' on the grounds of giving business more freedom, and allowing the market 'to have its head', has resulted in the biggest financial crash of our lifetime. By contrast, Quaker businessmen of the nineteenth century, such as Joseph Rowntree and John Cadbury, obeyed not just the law but their own code of responsibility towards the wider community. They saw themselves not as outright owners but as stewards, answerable to God for how they developed their businesses and treated their workers.

The need for formation, aimed at developing, deep within us, values which promote human flourishing, clear laws which protect the wider interests of society and accountability to that wider society, as well as to shareholders, has never been greater.

3.2.   STABILITY

Benedict has no time for 'gyrovagues' (*RSB* 1.10), monks who are always flitting from one place to another. So one of the Benedictine vows is stability, which in practice means agreeing to stay in the same community until you die, trying to get on with the people you are stuck with. Like marriage, it is for better and for worse. Christopher Jamieson, the former Abbot of Worth, adds an important observation to this. He says: 'The people you find most difficult are the ones who will teach you most about yourself.'[4] That is, of course, assuming you are actually looking to learn about yourself, rather than thinking how much better life would be if that other person would change—or just disappear, to put it politely.

But, as Rowan Williams reminded the Church when it was discussing the thorny issue of women bishops, the people we don't agree with are not going away.[5] And indeed, if they did our lives would be much the poorer for it. Do we really want to live in a monochrome world where everybody is just like us? So, we need a stable base, a place of commitment, of solid relationships, where we can learn and struggle and work through the difficulties and grow together into something deeper, something more profound, something better. John Lennon and Paul McCartney just couldn't get on with each other; in the end they split up. But the quality of their work on their own was nothing compared to the electric brilliance that sparked off between them when they stuck together.

Stability is something of huge significance for us in the twenty-first century western world because stability is something we have lost, and in a very big way. I was brought up in Leeds. My extended

family, about 25 of us, all lived within a one mile radius of each
other in the middle of Leeds. We were in and out of each other's
homes all the time. We had big Christmas parties at my Grandma
and Granddad Topham's at 1 Tanfield Street. That's all gone now,
swept away by University expansion and inner city motorways.
None of us live there anymore. The older generations are mostly
dead, and my generation and my children's generation are gone
to the four winds—Kidderminster, Ely, Liverpool, London, Spain,
Germany, Australia. We didn't plan it that way. It just happened.
It's like Joni Mitchell's song 'Big Yellow Taxi': 'You don't know what
you've got 'til it's gone.' Well, it has gone! Mobility and a flexible job
market have certainly brought its benefits, but it has come at a price.

After my dad died, my mum became confused and increasingly
dependent. We were living in Cambridge and my only brother
lived in Germany. So, week after week, we were in the car, up the
A1 to Leeds. Many of my friends recount similar stories. It was
during this period that we visited our friends Eric and Adrine
in Uganda. As we arrived in their home village, the truck was
suddenly surrounded by people, over a hundred of them, from
children to the elderly. I asked Eric: 'How many of these people
are your relatives?' 'All of them,' he replied. Eric's mum, like my
own, was elderly, frail, and confused. However, in her case she
was surrounded by family caring for her personal needs, looking
after her crops, doing the cooking, or just sitting, chatting to her.
And it didn't all fall to a single person, as so often happens in the
West, but to the whole group. She remained at the centre of the
family, rather than isolated and apart from it. Most of us in the
West have now lost those support structures which, 50 years ago,
we took for granted.

Good, long-term relationships are like money in the bank—
except that it doesn't operate a credit system, so you can't cash
in what you haven't got. Sooner or later it catches up with you.
You set up home in a new place with great new jobs. You both
commute to London, earn good money and enjoy the lifestyle.
Then you have your first baby. The pregnancy is difficult and leaves
you exhausted. The baby, lovely as she is, isn't well and is up every

night for months. You become increasingly frazzled, ratty with one another and struggling to cope. You thought you'd go back to work after three months but that doesn't seem possible at present and you start to feel the squeeze financially. Your parents live 200 miles away and so do all those mates, who you haven't had time to keep up with anyway. You don't really know anybody locally, and there is no one you can turn to for help. Each of us could supply similar examples from our own experience.

And it is not just at a personal level. My dad worked all his life, apart from the war years in the Navy, for the same firm. It engendered a huge sense of loyalty and pride. Indeed, much of the success of Japanese companies after the War can be traced to the worker/company understanding of secure jobs for life, and the huge loyalty and hard work that gave rise to. Stability has economic value. If you don't believe that, just look at the relationship between Steve Job's health and the Apple share price. And how often do you hear businessmen talk about the need for stable trading conditions when they are thinking about where to invest?

But stability, in the old sense of the word, has gone, and there is no putting the genie back in the bottle. We will not return to living in villages where we are related to half the community, nor to single-industry towns which employed half the population, but that doesn't mean we can't find stability. There are many examples in the business world of strong companies, such as John Lewis, with dedicated workforces which have been with them for years, often people who themselves have shares in the company, and therefore a vested interest in its long-term success, rather than in earning a quick buck and moving on, hang the consequences.

But just as Obedience can be abused, so can stability. It's so easy for institutions to become closed and unwelcoming to outsiders. My 'stability' can be your 'exclusion'. That is why hospitality is such an important theme for Benedict, who draws from the many Bible stories on that theme.

Stable communities, open to new ideas and new people, are essential for human flourishing. They do not treat human beings like dispensable commodities. Stability is part of the recipe for economic flourishing.

3.3.   TRANSFORMATION

The sayings of the Desert Fathers are full of pithy wisdom. Here is one of them:

> Abbot Lot came to Abbot Joseph and said: 'Father, according as I am able I keep my little rule, and my little fast, my prayer, my meditation and contemplative silence; and according as I am able I strive to cleanse my heart of evil thoughts: now, what more should I do?' The elder rose up in reply and stretched out his hands to heaven, and his fingers became like ten lamps of fire. He said: 'Why not be totally changed into fire?'[6]

The Benedictine vow of Conversatio Morum is perhaps best understood as 'transformation', not settling for where you are, but being willing to go on being changed, again and again, however uncomfortable that may be. God calls Abraham to step out into the unknown and says to him: 'Through you all the families of the earth shall be blessed.' (cf. Genesis 12.3, NIV) But that very soon turns into: 'Through God, me and all my loved ones shall be blessed.' It is so easy to be lost in our own small world. The whole point of our obedience and stability is to build a solid rock, not as a place where we can lock ourselves in and hide from the storm, but from which we can launch out, with a big vision, beyond our own small hopes and dreams, to make a difference in the world, for the better. The Rule of Taizé exhorts us: 'Never stand still, go forward with your brethren, run towards the goal in the footsteps of Christ.'[7]

At first sight this seems to be in conflict with Benedict's call to stability. Yet, in fact, the two go hand in hand. They need each other. Without transformation, stability produces an outmoded institution that cannot survive in a rapidly changing world. But without stability, transformation is rootless and in danger of creating havoc, as we have witnessed only too clearly in the current banking crisis, with people who have no long-term investment in the well-being of the organizations they work for, much less wider society, taking reckless gambles for short-term gains.

This commitment to transformation, rooted in a stable base with clear rules for all to follow, has all the potential to promote human creativity and flourishing. It is about being made in the image of God, who is endlessly creative and inventive. It is also central to the greatest achievements of humankind—in the arts, architecture, engineering, science, technology and medicine. And all these things are in turn dependent on economics, on investment and on business.

Obedience, Stability, Transformation: a framework for flourishing. A framework in which all three need to be present in order that we might flourish. A framework for flourishing not just for ourselves, not just for the companies we are involved with in public or private sector, but for society as a whole, for the common good of all, that the Kingdom of God might, indeed, become a reality on earth, as it is in heaven.

SUMMARY

- The vows of Obedience, Stability and Transformation are the foundations of the Benedictine 'Rule of Life'
- Obedience requires establishing working practices and values which promote responsible stewardship, accountability and a sense of mutual ownership
- Stability is about the long-term commitment rather

than making a quick buck. It promotes stable, solid relationships and structures in which people can feel secure enough to dream dreams and see them become reality

- Transformation is not settling for where we are, but constantly seeking to change, to push the boundaries and to develop our full potential, individually and corporately.
- Stability, Obedience and Transformation are not individual options, but belong together to produce a 'framework for flourishing' in all aspects of life, commercial as well as personal

NOTES

1. The quotation at the head of the chapter is a paraphrase of two provisions in Chapter 58 of the *Rule of St Benedict* (*RSB*), which sets out how new members of the monastic community are to be received. In David Parry's translation they read: 'All the things that are hard and repugnant to nature in the way to God are to be expounded to him . . . The one who is to be accepted into the community must promise in the oratory, in the presence of all, stability, conversion of life and obedience.' (*RSB* 58.8 & 17).

2. *Conversatio Morum* is usually rendered as 'conversion of life', which needs to be understood as a promise to conform to the spirit of the monastic life. Cardinal Basil Hume summed it up thus: '[It] commits the monk to a celibate life, to renounce personal ownership, and by constant effort to pursue those virtues essential to the monastic life and his service of God.' (Basil Hume, OSB, *In Praise of Benedict* (London: Hodder, 1996), pp.12, 13.

3. Esther de Waal, *Seeking God* (London: Fount, 1984), p. 43.

4. Abbot Christopher Jamison is quoted from the BBC television series *The Monastery.*

5. Archbishop Rowan Williams, *Presidential Address*, General Synod of the Church of England, 2009.

6. *The Wisdom of the Desert*, trans Thomas Merton (New York: Shambhala, 1960), p. 85
7. *Rule of Taizé*, Preamble (Les Presses de Taize, 1968). The Taizé Community is an international, ecumenical monastic community, near Maçon in France.

4. HUMAN AND FINANCIAL VALUE

— Rosie Harper & Alan Wilson —

*What kind of deal is it to get everything
you want but lose yourself? What could
you ever trade your soul for?*
MATTHEW 16.26 (MV)

Christianity is the most materialistic of religions. It begins with God creating a material world and loading it up with the good that is to be found in everything. But clearly we do not seem to be experiencing that good in the way we do economics. Recent experiences are just the tip of the iceberg. Throughout human history the way we have handled money has been an agent for both great good and extraordinary levels of oppression. If we are to pose the question 'Is there a different Christian way to operate in the realm of finance?' we need to explore both the theological foundations on which we might build an answer, and be bold enough to step into the real world and express what a different way might look like, beyond the theoretical.

The foundation of all Christian understanding is that the Word of God, the source of all life and meaning, found expression in human form in the person, life and teaching of Jesus of Nazareth. This affirms both the actuality and the goodness of human living. Christians have not always grasped this. There was once a student who was a very genuine, if pious, Christian. His understanding of a redeemed way of viewing money was to give away his grant at the beginning of term. His Christian friends then had to house and feed him, and as they did so they experienced his naïveté as manipulative. Far from suggesting that the Christian way should be removed from the messy business of everyday living, its core tradition rejects any dualism or tendency to write off the visible world as contemptible. St Paul, looking forward, pictures a whole creation subjected to futility, but groaning in travail as it awaits its redemption, a glorious and complete liberty that touches everything God has made, and in which he delights (cf. Romans 8.18–23) The Church is no more than the first fruits of this harvest that will include everything of real worth on the day God is all in all. So there is no escape from material goods, and no evading the notion that they are good. Jesus tells us, 'I came that they may have life, and may have it in all its fullness.' (John 10.10).

It should come as no surprise, then, that a large amount of Jesus' teaching concerns money. He sees it as a poor indicator of worth, but a clear window into the soul. If economics is to be understood as a science of scarcity, then Jesus' richer teaching about wealth is a response to God's generosity in Creation, twenty-fold, forty-fold, a hundred-fold.[1]

Money itself is a mere system of counters. It has value as a servant, but not as a master. It is possible for rich people to feel poor and for poor people to feel rich. Mere calculation, like the fear of scarcity, is a mental construct created and held in people's minds alongside, but separate from the fullness of human reality. Jesus teaches that people, even rich fools, are infinitely more valuable than their wealth. Indeed the value of their goods is related not only to their amount of specie, but also to its human worth. In one of his sayings, Jesus remarked on a poor widow who had made a donation of two small coins to the Temple in Jerusalem; it was all she had to live on, and was a more generous gift than the large donations of the wealthy. (Mark 12.41–44) In God's economy the widow's mite is held to be more precious than the excess wealth of the rich.

If raw economic logic sees the world as a place of scarcities, Jesus sees the Kingdom—the world where God's rule prevails—as a place of sufficiency, if only people would accept it as such. More than that, if you confuse material gain with real worth you have deceived yourself. 'What kind of a deal is it to get everything you want but lose yourself? What could you ever trade your soul for?' (Matthew 16.26, MV) Hebrew prophets like Amos proclaimed that money is supposed to be a tool for liberation, not a means of oppression.

You cannot calculate how it is should be used by mere reckoning. Money is energy, not stuff. To absolutise money regardless of its human impact and significance leads to a kind of three-card trick. The cash value that can be mathematically assigned to money is logically, but not humanly, absolute. The fact that it has been calculated mathematically could make it look absolute. Treating it is though it were makes it a source of power and oppression—an easy pairing to grasp for any who had experienced first-century tax gathering in full swing.

Absolutizing the value of the money in someone's wallet over and above the person whose wallet it is, just because it can be reckoned mathematically, reduces the human being. They become no more than a means to an end. A system of oppression founded on materialism then protects itself by abusing anyone who disagrees with this comparative valuation, or suggests we do in fact have a choice in the matter, by condemning them as a starry-eyed idealist, flying in the face of absolute economic reality.

The truth, Jesus implies, is that we are free to set all kinds of different values on goods and services depending on how much they matter to us. Jesus' parable of the Workers in the Vineyard makes the point well. The owner of a vineyard recruits casual workers at various times of the day, agreeing with each one what they will be paid. At the end of the day, when the wages are paid, each receives the agreed amount, but this turns out to be the same for all irrespective of whether they have worked a full day or just one hour. To the complaints of those who have worked the longest, the owner replies that he has treated them fairly. They have received a full day's wage, and should not complain because he chooses to be generous towards others who only worked for a short time. (Matthew 20.1–16) The owner chose to set the value of each worker at a days' sufficiency regardless of the actual hours worked. He is acting justly in paying each worker equally, because in God's eyes we are all of equal worth. The workers who put in long hours see this as unjust because they need to feel of greater worth than their neighbours. The radical rounding up involved requires calculation, but the will that drives it is beyond mere reason. In the

Kingdom you get paid not according to the scarcity of your labour, the amount of work to be done, or even the employer's wealth, but the amount you need to be able to participate with dignity and joy in the community. If you truly understood real sufficiency as a gift of grace, you would, perhaps, want no more.

The concept of gracious sufficiency challenges the attitudes of overly materialistic rich people. Poor people in the first century Middle East had, of course, hardly any choice in the matter, moral or otherwise. One central message of Jesus' teaching is that the rich, unlike the poor, are burdened by eternally significant decisions— how they deal with their wealth, especially how they respond to the needs of the poor. How they choose to manage their riches now should be consistent with their hopes hereafter, governed by two key concepts:

1. The rich need to understand that God expects anyone to have sufficient for their dignity, but not extra to set themselves above their poorer neighbours. They may consider themselves to have some superior entitlement but God does not. He sets the higher value on everyone.

2. Jesus cuts across all assumptions the rich may make about their own value. A banker is no more a wealth-creator than the nurse who saves his life in Casualty, and no less. Nobody needs to beggar their neighbour in order to achieve sufficiency. The notion that somehow you deserve ludicrously more than you could ever spend is not a sign of blessing, as some practitioners of the so-called prosperity gospel might imply, because it is not based on true wealth, but an absurd accumulations of specie that betokens pathological spiritual bankruptcy.   *coinage*

There is, indeed, no one-to-one correlation between amounts of money and human value. Ask any urban vicar who then moved out to a more prosperous parish. Personally, it is a transition from being near the top to near the bottom of the financial pecking order. You would need four of the fivers that meant everything to a neighbour in the school playground, fighting to make ends meet for her family at the end of the week, to buy a raffle ticket in the affluent suburbs. What comparative value can be set upon it?

Setting a paramount value upon each human life, as a gift of God, not only relieves the rich from defining themselves by their goods, it also delivers the poor from defining their value by their material poverty. It gives everyone dignity as the people they are by the life they have, not the money they do or do not possess. In our current political atmosphere there is a strong shift towards only targeting resources towards the 'deserving' poor. Those who are deemed unemployed because of their own indolence, or those who are sick because of their own foolishness are stripped of their value and, it is suggested, are not worthy of society's support. Our Christian bedrock of grace would suggest otherwise.

Many people reduced to circumstances of extreme poverty lose all interest in the riches of others, seeing them as unattainable. Only a belief in their own worth, and the possibility of a grace that cannot be taken away from them offers hope and thus a basis upon which to believe their circumstances could change. The poor may be free to climb a ladder of economic advancement, but it only delivers them to a better place if it can be done without compromising their ability to lead a good and worthwhile life. Until human beings are free from defining themselves in money terms, they will unfailingly underestimate their true worth, along with everybody else's. They will set themselves over and against others, compromising their ability to receive friendship and other relational wealth for what it is, with a thankful heart.

Equality turns out to be the only basis upon which true joy can be founded. If we build friendships upon anything other than a radical acceptance of equality between ourselves, founded on thankfulness for our shared humanity as a gift, we may be able in this life to live out our fantasy, but it remains a fantasy, as Jesus made plain in the parable of Dives and Lazarus (Luke 16.19–31). Dives (which means 'riches') lived and feasted in great magnificence, ignoring the needs of the poor man, Lazarus, who, covered in sores, scratched out a living at his gate. When Dives dies he finds himself in the torments of hell, paying the price for his lack of humanity. The message is clear: in the end there will be no hiding place from the God-given equality that was not acknowledged in this life. To play inequality games founded on finance impoverishes everyone.

In another parable Jesus pictured a rich man whose land had yielded heavy crops, so much so that he had a problem storing all that he had gained. He built new barns to store his excess, and said to himself, '[Man], you have plenty of good things laid by, enough for many years to come: take life easy, eat drink and enjoy yourself.' But God said to him, 'You fool, this very night you must surrender your life; and the money you have made—who will get it now?' (Luke 12.13–21). As we lie on our deathbeds only a very few of us will be obsessing about who gets what, something we can only do if our goods have been exerting too great a claim upon us. When we die and lose all control over everything, our illusion will be exposed for the fatuity it always was.

If the first serious encounter we have with the radical reality of human equality is powerlessness in the face of disease and death, we will be terribly surprised when, as is inevitable, they come calling for us at the last. The years we may have spent accumulating, buttressing an ultimately fatuous inequality, will scarce fit us for the heartbreaking reality of that hour. Christ on the cross remains Son of God with everything stripped from him and the thieves hanging by his side—a radical form of equality in its own right. When he said to the dying thief, ' today you will be with me in paradise,' (Luke 23.43) the hope that Jesus held out was offered completely free, unencumbered by any transactional price tag or, indeed, tangible effect. It was an image of pure grace working through faith founded on love—a left-handed, entirely non-transactional hope. It is this death, the most profound witness of our equality and God's grace, which underpins the Christian imperative to found our understanding of economics on such equality.

Hans Kung goes further and argues that this underlying principle should be convincing to all, religious or not. More than that, he equates treating people with economic equity in the same category as all other basic human rights:

> ... every human being must be treated humanely ...
> This means that every human being without distinction
> of age, sex, race, skin colour, physical or mental ability,
> language, religion, political view, or national or social
> origin possesses an inalienable and untouchable dignity ...
> Humans ... must be ends, never mere means, never objects
> of commercialization and industrialization in economic,
> politics and media.[2]

It is, in radically heightened form, the wisdom by which Jesus reminded his hearers how futile it is to give dinners if all you are after is an invitation back. This is partly because such a transactional game, in itself, evacuates the word 'give' of any gracious effect.

So what does believing in radical equality rooted in grace imply about money?

It liberates the rich from status anxiety and the poor from abject hopelessness. There is no longer any need for anyone to pretend they are anything they are not, or to stake their value on winning the lottery or hoarding their cash. Grounding identity in grace liberates people from fear of the inevitable equality that waits in the grave. Should the angel come tonight for your soul, as one night she will, you could leave free from regrets, recriminations or the folly of false grandeur.

When Jesus said the poor were blessed he could be thought to be idealising or romanticising poverty. But he goes on, paradoxically, to say they inherit the earth. This does not mean that some day they will win the lottery using a ticket from the gutter, but that they already have inherent value, a human wealth, beyond all calculation. When human rather than monetary value is placed at the centre of all calculation, grace and sufficiency are enacted, and there is no longer any need to be driven by fear or greed. Mere shortages are not the final word. Those who fail to see this and stake everything on selfish gain part company with reality and run the risk of missing life itself.

Many Christians grasp this and live lives of extraordinary generosity and integrity. The challenge to enact what we believe as a part of the economic life of our society is always uncomfortable. When the media shout 'It's the economy stupid' at every election how do we articulate a different way? What we actually do, how we vote, which shares we buy, which economic ideology we work with—all this turns into the daily experience of life for us all and especially for the least powerful.

Decisions about money are probably the most morally crucial that human beings make . . . it is the use of money, more than anything else, that affects people's lives for good or ill. Decisions about money are not only those which affect our personal life . . . No less important are the decisions made by companies and governments. These decisions are literally matters of life and death for billions of people on earth.[3]

SUMMARY

- The world as God created it is good and has an inherent generous sufficiency.
- The way we all experience it as good is related to the way we value one another and the world's resources.
- Money is a mere system and only has value as a servant, not a master.
- Jesus relates the use of money to grace, giving each person what they need because of who they are not what they do.
- In death lies our ultimate equality.
- Enacting that equality becomes a practical, not a theoretical, imperative for the Christian.

NOTES

1. The point about God's generosity in creation refers to the parable of the Sower (Mark 4.1–9) in which Jesus likens God's generosity to an abundant harvest where the yield might be thirtyfold, sixtyfold, or even a hundredfold.

2. Hans Küng and Karl-Josef Kuschel (eds.), *A Global Ethic*, (SCM Press; London, 1993), p. 23.

3. The quotation is from Richard Harries, *The Re-enchantment of Morality* (SPCK; London, 2008), p. 108.

5.   TRUST

— **Richard Backhouse** —

He who is shrewd in business will prosper,
but happy is he who puts his trust in the Lord.
PROVERBS 16.20

In the series of programmes by Michael Blastland in March 2011
for the More or Less slot on BBC Radio 4, Paul Seabright spoke
about early trade encounters, in particular trading between Libyans
and Carthaginians. One party would put their goods on the
ground, retreating to a safe distance while the potential purchasers
examined them (the vendors surreptitiously cutting off escape
routes in case the buyers tried to abscond). The buyers would lay
down the goods they proposed to exchange and retreat in turn to
guard the exit routes. And so the process would go on, until both
parties were satisfied, when exchange was made. Thus both parties
were able to mitigate, but never eliminate, risks in their exchange.

Trust is an underpinning necessity of all transactions, as is
illustrated by the anecdote above. In that case, each group risks
the other group seeking to make an escape with both sets of goods
offered for sale. Similarly, trust is exercised when an employee is
hired, when livestock is sold, or when land is bought. The trust
required may be that the payment is genuine, or it may be that
the goods are what they appeared to be, or it may even be that
the goods really did belong to the seller before the sale was made.

The level of trust apparently required for exchange, at least
in relatively primitive markets, perhaps helps us to understand
why humans are the only species to undertake transactions. If to
transact is to trust, and to trust is human, then one might argue
that to transact is to be human. Not all transactions are the same.
An early observation about transactions was made by Aristotle. He
drew a clear distinction between the 'value in use' and the 'value

in exchange' of the goods involved in a transaction. A shoe sold to be worn has 'value in use'. In such a case, providing the use of the shoe yields enough utility to the buyer, and the payment enough compensation to the seller, then the transaction can take place on the basis of trust: each party believes that the transaction is worthwhile to them, and that the other is not 'getting one over on them'. However, if the object has only, or even principally, 'value in exchange', and is being used as a commodity to be bought at a low price and sold at a profit, then the vendor may be mistrustful—could they not obtain the higher price for themselves? What information does the buyer hold which makes them willing to offer a price acceptable to the vendor in confidence of obtaining a higher price elsewhere? Aristotle was suspicious of transactions which were predicated on the goods' 'value in exchange'. Indeed, he described such transactions as 'unnatural'.

In reality, however, most transactions, whether they involve 'value in use' or 'value in exchange' take place in an environment of risk. Of course, higher risk affects the trust paradigm on which transactions might be based. One cause of higher risk in transactions is asymmetric information. An imbalance of information arises when the product is sufficiently complex, or sufficiently hard to inspect, that the vendor is in a significantly better position to understand the value of the product. In his famous 1970 article,[1] Akerlof explained why all second-hand cars would be 'lemons' (i.e., poor quality vehicles), which has become the classic economist's illustration of this problem (although it has many applications). Akerlof suggested that, if second-hand car buyers cannot tell whether they are buying a 'cherry' (an excellent condition car) or a 'lemon', they will never offer a price better than that of a 'lemon'. In turn, if buyers will never offer more than this, sellers, realising that they cannot obtain a price better than that of a 'lemon', will never offer such a 'cherry' for sale second-hand. The expectation of 'lemon' prices brings only 'lemons' onto the market. And there can be no second-hand car market for 'cherries', or a very limited one at best.

In the case of Akerlof's second-hand car market, the market is dysfunctional, and it is dysfunctional because a basis for trust—that purchaser and vendor can equally validate the quality of the product on inspection—is absent. In fact the asymmetric information, as well as making one market dysfunctional (the market for 'lemons'), it also prevents another market from working at all—that for 'cherries'. Akerlof's model might also explain one reason why Christians put Icthus stickers (the Greek for 'fish') on the back of their cars. When the time comes to sell their car, they expect others to read this market signal of honesty, and give them a price closer to that of a 'cherry' than a 'lemon'. This was certainly the thinking of one friend of mine, who, whilst a stranger to church, would always buy an Ichthus sticker for his car when he came to sell it, because he believed it added several hundred pounds to the sale price. Indeed, it might help a sale to take place where no sale would be possible, because it provided a basis for trust (misplaced, in my friend's case) between buyer and seller.

In health markets, Akerlof's work was applied to suggest that health insurance will only be sought by the unhealthy, therefore health insurers will find that they have a biased sample of the population applying for health insurance—in effect, they are the ones buying the 'lemons'. Rationally, one might expect health insurance markets to fail, or to end up charging much higher prices than an objective assessment of probabilities might suggest. Those with an expectation that their need for health care would make them 'cherries' in Akerlof's model, would avoid the market altogether until such time as a re-evaluation made them think of themselves as 'lemons'.

All these examples assume of course that every transaction is a 'one-shot game'. In Chapter 9, Nick Bion suggests that the building up of trust in a transactional relationship (in which transactions are expected to be repeated) is an important Christian response. It is, however, also a rational response: a rationalist might suggest that a trading relationship becomes worth investing in, and this dilutes the need to maximise utility, or profit, from each individual transaction, maybe suggesting that the vendor may be less cautious with adverse information, in order to encourage repeat business.

In the theo-economy, such expectation of relationship with the customer (and maybe, therefore, repeat custom) could result in a simple and straightforward expectation of honesty on both sides (although one might rationalise this by suggesting that, where moral probity is more highly valued, a single alleged moral lapse would contaminate one's commercial reputation even more severely). Nevertheless, if one would expect a theo-economy to be one in which the agents sought to 'love their neighbour as themselves', it would be reasonable to expect this and thereby seek to build up trust through honesty and straight-dealing because there was relationship, rather than merely transaction. If this takes place, one significant consequence would be to mitigate, if not obviate, the adverse results of asymmetric information. In fact, trust may become a substitute for any information which is lacking. In the same way that we might expect, where a second-hand car salesman is selling to a direct relative, the buyer-relative would be directed away from the 'lemons' on their forecourt, and towards the 'cherries'; the participant in the theo-economy would reveal which of the cars on their forecourt were in good condition on the un-inspectable inside, rather than merely on the outside. The individual seller, by revealing all the details of their own experience of ownership of the car, would reveal exactly where on the spectrum from a 'cherry' to a 'lemon' their own vehicle lies.

Trust has therefore a vital role to play in the economy: there are clear circumstances where its substitute, information, cannot be utilized. The theo-economy could form, in some way, a model for economies, if it represents the way in which trust can be restored into trading relationships. If one were to examine the (much more local) economy of the late eighteenth century, one might find that transactions taking place in small towns within the context of permanent relationships were able to exhibit high levels of trust. The modern economy has lost, or at least mislaid, the context for such trust in trade.

It is worth reflecting on why the modern economy, for all it resembles perfect competition, has so reduced trust between its agents. Perhaps it is exactly because markets have been encouraged to resemble perfect competition in so many regards—because this has reduced relationship in transaction. Furthermore two social revolutions have accelerated the depersonalization of modern transactions: the move to out-of-town superstores, and e-tailing. The first reduces even the purchase of groceries, which we might expect to be regular enough for relationship to develop (as once it did), to a mere transaction. Observe how little conversation takes place between the checkout operator and the purchaser at a supermarket, and compare it to the experience of Mary Portas, who, when buying meat from her local butcher (for her family after her mother died) on her way home from school, would find that he had already prepared what she needed, so that she did not even need to ask.[2] Such personal service, such customer-seller relationship, is rare in the modern, supermarket economy.

In the second place, e-tailing accelerates the same process. Can one develop a relationship of trust with Amazon, particularly when it acts as a portal through which other e-tailers operate? Online auction houses have used feedback scores to create a barometer of trust for those entering into transactions with unknown people. Whilst this is better than nothing, it is difficult to equate feedback scores giving a 92% positive rating with the trust that might arise with repeated transactions in the physical economy. The irony is surely that the internet was supposed to bring perfect competition a little closer. Instead, like the social and planning changes than ran ahead of it, the web has helped us to realize that perfect competition is not so perfect: it only works if perfect information can replace the trust that is lost. The quantity of buyers and sellers which perfect competition implies (or requires) suggests that relationship and trust are impossible; in a world with huge numbers of tiny buyers and sellers in which buyers can genuinely exercise choice between all sellers, how would a relationship develop? Thus the economy can only rely on the buyer being able to be sufficiently well-informed about the product that they are not vulnerable to inadvertently purchasing a 'lemon'. And, since an atomized market has no means of developing relationships and trust, the modern 'depersonalised economy' becomes one in which brands are trusted (or not) rather than people.

Even on a small scale, and in a theo-economy, could trust replace the need for perfect information? If the buyer was concerned with the seller gaining a win, and the seller concerned with the buyer 'winning', would other-person centredness allow transactions to take place? The rationalist would, once again, argue that it is no different from the desire so to satisfy the customer that they become repeat buyers. There is a reasonable basis to expect therefore that a theo-economy would, or could, be accompanied by complete openness in information. If buyers could entirely trust sellers, then the price would, in and of itself, constitute disclosure of all relevant information. Trust would mean that the most ignorant of car-buyers could purchase a second-hand car without the attendant surveys or warranties. Within small communities, such as kibbutzim, in which relationships are long term and assured, this may already happen.

Perhaps the greatest challenge of the modern economy is to preserve trust, and the most vulnerable markets would be those in which purchasers were least likely to be repeat buyers. This would suggest that the theo-economy would experience dysfunction in markets for housing, second-hand cars, or holidays much more than it might in milk, fresh flowers, or newspapers. Or, indeed, it may be that the mortgage-market, and that for savings, are most vulnerable. Recent history would suggest so.

How would the theo-economy deal with Akerlof's theory as it is applied to health markets? Could the example of Boaz encourage a theonomic society in which the community takes responsibility for the individual?[3] The local community, or *ecclesia*, ought already to be doing so. The fact that the modern hospice movement had its origin in Christian organizations suggests that the ability of faith communities, particularly Christian ones, to care for the less, or least, fortunate in society by voluntary subscription is hardly new. In fact, the modern equivalent of St Paul's collection for believers in Jerusalem from believers throughout the Roman empire forms an encouraging example of what can be achieved when, in trust, Christians seek to collaborate to provide not only for the own interests but also those of others. Here the modern economy, via compulsory taxation and the National Health Service in the UK, has provided a model of Christian behaviour. In this aspect of the theo-economy, the Christian has only to, '. . . render unto Caesar . . . ' (Nick Bion makes a similar point in Chapter 9.) Taxation can fulfil, in part at least, the social function once undertaken by the Temple in Israel, and the early Church in the Roman Empire. But like the relationship with a large company, the taxpayer has to trust the government to use the money well to provide a good product. Big government, like big markets, is not conducive to such trust in the way that communities were, and are.

SUMMARY

- Trust is an underpinning necessity of all transactions
- Most transactions take place in an environment of risk, and risk is increased the more asymmetric the information possessed by the parties.
- But where a relationship has been established between seller and buyer, for example through repeated transactions, it would be rational to expect that trust would increase and overcome the adverse results of asymmetric of information.
- In a theo-economy, the presence of trust would be the normal expectation even in one-off transactions, and this offers a model for economies.
- In the modern economy trust has been reduced because relationship in transaction has been reduced, particularly by the move to out-of-town superstores and e-tailing: both depersonalise transactions.
- The great challenge of the modern economy is to preserve trust.

NOTES

1. George A. Akerlof, 'The Market for "Lemons": Quality Uncertainty and the Market Mechanism', *Quarterly Journal of Economics,* vol. 84 (August 1970), pp. 488–500.

2. Mary Portas is an English businesswoman, retail expert and broadcaster, best known for her retail and business-related television shows, and most recently appointed by the Government to lead a review of the future of Britain's high streets. (Wikipedia)

3. Boaz is one of the main characters in the Book of Ruth. His compassion for Ruth, an impoverished relative, resulted in his taking responsibility for ensuring her future security.

6. LEADERSHIP, ETHICS & VIRTUE: USING THE RULE OF ST BENEDICT AS A MODEL FOR LEADERSHIP

— Peter Sills —

Let God's house be wisely cared for by wise men.
ST BENEDICT OF NURSIA[1]

6.1. THE ETHICAL DEFICIT

We kid ourselves if we think that the financial crisis is the result of bad banking arrangements, bad luck in investment decisions, or misguided fiscal policy. These matters, and more besides, had their part to play, but at root the cause is human failure. Banking systems are designed by people, investment decisions are made by people, and fiscal policies are determined by people. This seems to have been conveniently ignored. Since the crisis began in 2007 official responses have been about improving systems, not about improving the people who operate them. Indeed, as has been pointed out many times, the systems are adequate (apart from allowing the union of retail and investment banking); it is those who operated them who failed to use their powers adequately, and it was their perception of what was ethically appropriate, as distinct from what was lawful, that was at fault. There really is no such thing as a financial crisis pure and simple; there is always a more basic moral or ethical crisis, and more than four years later we wait for this dimension to be publicly recognised, let alone acted upon. For too long moral discussion in the public sphere has been about designing systems to avoid problems recurring and about adopting codes of ethics—usually admirable in conception, but ineffective in operation. As Al Gini, Professor of Business Ethics, Loyola University, Chicago, has said, 'Business ethics' and 'ethical leadership' are two glaring examples of academic oxymorons.[2] Lots of evidence supports the notion that ethics can impede a successful career, that bending the rules is commonplace, and what characterises the management sets the tone for the whole enterprise, the workforce following suit. Indeed ethics were definitely not allowed to impede the careers of the financial management, as the Oscar-nominated film on the financial crisis, *Inside Job*, shows chillingly. In particular, it shows how little leading financiers and economists evaluate options, new products and conduct in moral terms. It is an appalling exposé of the lack of a moral compass in the financial sector. The financial deficit is paralleled by an equally serious moral deficit, and this is seen also in other areas of life: MP's expenses, phone hacking and routine cheating in the premier league, to take three of the more glaring examples.

Even where we do know what is ethically right and wrong, and how to design regulatory systems, it is apparent that we do not know is how to 'design' people with the appropriate internal moral values and the necessary strength of character to operate those systems, and, more importantly, to do the right thing when the system fails or where there is no system. Setting the right standards and ensuring compliance is one of the basic functions of leadership; so also is the formation of good character in those who are led, and this, of course, requires attention to matters beyond any system or policy. It requires attention to who we are in the depths of our being, to the values and attitudes that motivate us and give us a sense of purpose and worth. This is, of course, one of the basic tasks of religion, and, in large part, our moral vision has atrophied because we have abandoned and rejected our Christian heritage, the historic source of the moral framework of both our public and private lives. It would be naive to suppose that the financial crisis will lead us to re-embrace our Christian heritage, but there are models of ethical leadership to hand that draw on that heritage, in particular that of St Benedict of Nursia. He offers a way in which the moral framework can be re-accessed, and in a way that speaks to those of all faiths and of none. His wisdom is basic to understanding the moral nature of leadership.

6.2.   CHARACTER & VIRTUE

Benedict's teaching on leadership is, of course, within the context of a monastic community. Central to the well-being of the community is its leader, the Abbot, and central to his role is character formation. The Abbot's concern is not to develop in his monks practical skills and aptitudes, but rather, and above all, the strength of character that enables them to live according to their highest aspirations. As Al Gini has argued, character is the most crucial and most elusive element of leadership. The English word is rooted in the Greek word for engraving, and just as the engraver produces a permanent mark on metal, so character refers to the permanent marks or 'etched-in factors' of our personality, both those we were born with and those that have come from our life and experience. It is these 'engravings' that define us, make us unique, and determine how we act. Benedict knew this, and chief among the marks that he wanted to define his monks was growth in virtue, and that is the key to the ethical formation of character.

Today's ethical deficit has produced various calls for a return to virtue; what is virtue? Virtue is not something we hear much about; people speak more about values, but the two are not the same. Values are the qualities and standards that we choose to live by or which shape our work. They are often conventional: they are not necessarily self-serving (though some may be, and self-serving values feature strongly in the ethical deficit), but, whatever their nature, we like to think our values are self-chosen, that values come from me. Virtue, by contrast is something given, an inner quality, a grace that enables us to live a life that is morally good. Virtue is prior to values, and the capacity for virtue, like love, is something that we are all born with, but it needs time to grow, and we have to learn how to express it. We might picture virtue as the fountain or well that is usually placed at the centre of the monastery cloister. The cloister is the inner space of the monastery around which its whole life revolves and which connects its various parts. Our inner life is also an enclosed space around which the whole of our life revolves and which connects its various parts, and virtue is like the fountain welling up inside it, nourishing it and giving it life. Virtue is the agent of inner change and growth, and the pursuit of virtue gives us the moral strength to live by higher qualities and standards than those that simply serve our self-interest.

In classical philosophy there are four cardinal virtues: prudence, temperance, fortitude, and justice, and they were described in Chapter 2. Rowan Williams has summarised them neatly:

> Prudence is good judgement; Temperance is emotional intelligence . . . understanding our desires and bringing them into self-critical awareness; Fortitude is courage . . . without being deflected by circumstance; and Justice is doing what is due to the individual, society and the environment.

Each of these virtues requires us to stand back from the immediate and to take a longer term view, and have regard for the common good. They remind us that there is a selfless quality to good leadership, and this is reflected in Benedict's frequent admonitions to the Abbot to be aware of his motives.

6.3.   THREE BASIC TASKS

These virtues are implicit in Benedict's approach to leadership. He does not systematise his teaching as we do today, but essentially it revolves around three basic tasks. These three tasks derive from the three vows that Benedictine monks take, stability, conversion of life and obedience, which Alan Hargrave discussed in Chapter 3). *Stability,* a commitment to a particular monastic community, means becoming rooted in the community; it is an open-ended commitment to seek your future with them, come what may, and this requires prudence and fortitude. *Conversion of life* is a promise to live according to the values of the community, and to let those values shape your life, particularly so that our lives serve a higher purpose than simply the fulfilment of our personal desires, wants and ambitions; this requires temperance. *Obedience,* accepting a source of authority outside of the self, means learning to grow in humility and learning to listen to voices other than our own, taking seriously the wisdom, experience, and common values of the community; this involves a concern for justice.

6.3.1.   Accountability

Building on these vows, the first task of the leader is to be accountable, and this derives from the vow of obedience. Time and again Benedict reminds the Abbot that, at the end of his life, he will have to give an account of his stewardship:

> The Abbot must always remember that at the fearful judgement of God two things will be discussed: his own teaching and the obedience of his disciples.
>
> **RSB *2.1, 6***

A lack of accountability is an important element in today's ethical deficit; it is particularly characteristic of charismatic and authoritarian leaders, who tend to act as if they are their own source of authority, able to dispense themselves from common principles of law and morality. Benedict also requires accountability among the members of the community; he placed upon the monks the obligation of mutual obedience:

> The goodness of obedience is not to be shown only through obedience to the Abbot, but the brethren should also obey each other . . .
>
> **RSB 71.1**

These two principles take the idea of accountability beyond formal lines of reporting—to superiors, shareholders, etc.—and also beyond institutional boundaries. Vertically, accountability stretches beyond the institution to a higher authority, whether conceived of as a divine being, common morality, personal conscience, or the public interest. Horizontally, accountability extends to colleagues, junior as well as senior, and to stakeholders and to the wider community. The absence of any higher notion of accountability is a major factor in today's economy: To whom were the bankers accountable? Did they acknowledge a higher duty, if not to God, then to the common good?

6.3.2.   Caring for Souls

The second task of the leader is caring for souls, and this derives from the vow of conversion of life:

> Let [the Abbot] always consider that it is souls that he has undertaken to rule, and for whom he will give an account.
>
> **RSB 2.34**

The word 'soul' is apt to be misunderstood: as used by Benedict it encapsulates our whole being, and particularly those qualities and attributes that distinguish humans from other creatures, so 'caring for souls' describes the leader's responsibility for the personal formation of those whom he leads. In secular terms we might describe this as a concern for the whole person, and it is promoted through programmes for continuous professional development and the like. Benedict, no doubt, would approve, but he would ask if these programmes go beyond improving competence and productive capacity to deepening a person's moral resources. This is important, because both incompetence and moral failure contributed to the present crisis: the banks behaved recklessly as professional bankers, and they were also morally culpable. But Benedict would go a step further. Personal development is worth doing not just because better trained, more skilled and more fulfilled workers produce better quality work and have higher levels of productivity, but because they become better people. From a Benedictine perspective, enabling personal growth, for its own sake, is one of the basic responsibilities of leaders. This might be described as the secular equivalent of conversion of life. To enable personal growth, the leader must be a teacher—it is notable how many times the Rule refers to this aspect of the Abbot's role; for example, the Abbot is to 'rule over his disciples with two kinds of teaching; that is to say, he must show forth all good and holy things by his words and even more by his deeds.' (*RSB* 2.11) There is no room for double standards, no division between words and deeds, nor between public and private conduct; morality is one.

6.3.3.   Forming Community

The third task of the leader is to form the community. As the poet John Donne said, 'No man is an island, entire of itself.'[3] Accountability and personal growth are not simply individual endeavours, but take place within a community, and the leader is responsible for creating that community. This task derives from the vow of stability. 'Community' is so overused that the word has been almost emptied of meaning. It is not something that arises of its own accord around those who happen to live or work in the same place. As Benedict knew well, forming a community requires hard work. Those who join in community make an open-ended promise to make a journey together come what may; but making the journey and forming the community are symbiotic. It is travelling together that enables the journey to be made, and it is perseverance in the journey that forms the community and helps it to grow. Community is about bonds that are not negotiated, it is not the result of a carefully worked out balance of interests; it has much more to do with establishing a common purpose and identity, binding people together at a deeper level than the material and the protection of common interests.

The moral dimension of community has to do with holding the memories that give us our identity and sense of purpose. A community is at heart a community of memory. Part of the communal memory is the identity and values of the enterprise, which are both held and safeguarded by the community, whether it be a monastery or a business. Community should help us to see ourselves as part of a larger story which continues to give meaning to our lives despite their ups and downs, and, from a Christian perspective, that story will not be about conquest and power but about the aims and hopes that bind us together. It is easy to see what this means in a monastery, but if the monastic insights about community are true, then the challenge to business and other organizations is to work out what it means for them. An answer was offered by Pope John Paul II in 1991:

> The purpose of a business firm is not simply to make a profit, but is to be found in its very existence as a *community of persons* who in various ways are endeavouring to satisfy their basic needs, and who form a particular group at the service of the whole of society. Profit is a regulator of the life of a business, but it is not the only one; *other human and moral factors* must also be considered which, in the long term, are at least equally important in the life of a business.[4]

Personal growth and a sense of usefulness are among the basic needs of the community, and are two of the 'other human and moral factors' that regulate the life of a business along with profit.

6.4.   PERSONAL QUALITIES

Anyone reading the Rule is bound to be struck by the huge authority that Benedict vests in the Abbot: he directs all aspects of the life of the monastery, and the last word is his, secured by the vow of obedience. But the more closely we read the more we see that he is considerably constrained in the way he exercises his powers. Benedict constantly reminds him of three things: that he is accountable to God, that there is a moral framework within which he must act, and that the monks are always to be treated as individuals and never as a category. The Abbot leads as a servant, not as a master; he is constrained by the whole moral teaching of the Bible, and he must show a special concern for those with particular needs. Benedict eschews uniformity of provision in favour of individual need, and he warns the Abbot that he 'must bear in mind the weakness of those in need and not the ill-will of the envious.' (*RSB* 55.20–21) These three constraints, together with the three basic tasks, lie at the heart of ethical leadership, and to lead in this way requires particular personal qualities.

Secular lists of leadership qualities include things like drive and self-management, the ability to think strategically, get things done, and work under pressure; being able to work with people, and to motivate and care for them. Benedict stresses rather different qualities: self-awareness, fairness, balance, collaboration, discretion and humility. These two lists are not incompatible, but they place the stress at different points; Benedict stresses the qualities that underpin ethical leadership.

Self-Awareness is essential in an ethical leader. Time and again Benedict reminds the Abbot that more is demanded of him to whom more is entrusted. He must know himself as others know him; correcting the actions of others should foster a critical self-awareness, and make him careful of his own state: 'And so, while he provides by his instructions for the amendment of others, he will be brought also to the amendment of his own faults.' (RSB 2.31; 39–40). He must govern by deeds, not words (RSB 2.12).

Fairness requires a leader's actions and decisions to show both integrity and consistency. Benedict reminds the Abbot that he must not let his personal preferences or the social status of the monks determine his decisions. Rank is to be determined by merit, not by status or seniority, and he should not pretend that he does not see the faults of offenders. Fairness demands that he must be both a tough master and a loving father. (RSB 2.16–26)

Balance is one the keynotes of the Benedictine life: Benedict's attitude is both measured and moderate. While Benedict is very clear about how things should be done, this does not lead to an obsessive or dictatorial approach. The various needs and considerations must be prudently weighed and a measured course taken. But achieving balance does not mean a 'hands off' approach, as though the leader were an umpire: the Abbot must be of profit to his brethren and not just preside over them. In striking the right balance some things are clear:

> He should always prefer mercy to judgement . . . Let him hate sin, let him love the brethren'; in rooting out wrongdoing he should not be too zealous, 'lest in removing the rust the pot is broken', and 'it should be his aim to be loved rather than feared.'
>
> **RSB 64.8, 10, 12, 15**

Balance also requires a personal prudence:

> Let him not be restless or anxious, not over-demanding or obstinate, not a perfectionist or full of suspicion, or he will never have any peace.
>
> **RSB 64.16**

Collaboration ensures that decisions are owned by the whole community, and guards against management according to the personal whims of the leader. Benedict requires the whole community to be consulted when anything important has to be decided, and this must include the youngest as they often have the best insights—a remarkable requirement in a patriarchal age! In less important matters, it suffices to consult only the senior monks. For Benedict, there is more to leadership than telling people what to do. Al Gini articulates a Benedictine approach when he argues that the vision and values of leadership must have their origin in the community of which both the leader and followers are part. As he says, the leader's vision will not motivate if the community does not share it, nor will plans be effective if they are devised by the leader alone, and, most importantly, however compelling and charismatic the leader may be, the community must not allow the leader's will to replace their own.

Discretion and compassion are essential qualities in an ethical leader. Time and again, Benedict sets out a principle and then leaves to the Abbot discretion over its implementation, often reminding him of the special concern he should have for the weaker brethren. Faults must be corrected, but with prudence and charity. The Rule exemplifies the cardinal virtue of prudence, the practical wisdom that achieves its aim and keeps everyone on board:

> In giving his instructions he should have forethought and consideration . . . let him be discerning and moderate . . . [and] settle everything with foresight and justice.
>
> **RSB 64.14, 17; 3.6**

Leadership is a finely-balanced act requiring a well-honed discretion; towards the end of the Rule Benedict nicely summarises his approach:

> [The Abbot] should so regulate everything that the strong may desire to carry more, and the weak are not afraid.
>
> **RSB 64.19**

Humility, more than any other quality, underlies ethical leadership, and, significantly, it is not one that figures in most secular lists. Humility is the doorway to your inner self, to that part of our character that connects and gives life to all the other parts. As we have already noted, 'humility' comes from the Latin *humus*, meaning earth. It is about being earthed, being in touch with what is real. Humility is an inner strength that comes from a true appreciation of who we are and where we stand, helping us to appreciate that things will not fall apart if we do not have our own way all the time. Not only is it an essential foundation for the cardinal virtues, it is also basic to the three tasks of leadership. Humility keeps the leader from becoming overbearing, and from believing that his/her ideas are the only ones with merit; it promotes self-awareness and self-criticism; it allows the talents and insights of others to be recognised, giving them space to make their contribution; and it promotes peace of mind.[5]

6.5.   CONCLUSION

Classical economics is based on the presupposition that people will act rationally in the pursuit of their self-interest. Acting in our self-interest may indeed be the default position, but human behaviour shows other motivations, among them justice and compassion, conformity and fashion. It is not just Christians who wish to emphasise the former and discourage the latter; the financial crisis shows the catastrophe that results from self-interested action that ignores justice and compassion and the common good, and which bases its ethics on what everyone else is doing, conforming simply to the morality and fashions of the crowd. True self-interest requires a long term perspective, durable institutions and relationships, and solid values. Repairing our economic deficit requires us also to repair our ethical deficit, and this requires leadership based on virtue. We have to replace ideas of leadership based on power or position with the understanding that it is a moral relationship founded on trust, commitment and a shared vision of the good.[6] Benedict helps us to understand the nature of this complex moral relationship, and what it requires of the leader. True self-interest requires leadership that will not forsake the care of souls for worldly advantage (cf. *RSB* 2.33).

SUMMARY

- The ethical deficit is the result of human failure rather than deficient systems of control.
- Equipping staff with the necessary moral strength of character to act ethically is an essential and basic function of leadership, requiring attention to who we are in the depths of our being.
- St Benedict offers a model of ethical leadership—a way in which the lost moral framework can be re-accessed—which speaks to those of all faiths and of none.
- Above all St Benedict stresses growth in virtue, namely, the capacity to live by values that are morally good; virtue is prior to values.
- The four cardinal virtues are prudence, temperance, fortitude and justice.
- Consistent with these virtues, the three basic tasks of the ethical leader are: to be accountable, to care for the whole person, and to form the community.
- The leader's powers need to be exercised within a clear moral framework, and people are always to be treated as individuals, never as a category.
- In contrast to secular lists of leadership qualities, the qualities that underlie ethical leadership are: self-awareness, fairness, balance, collaboration, discretion and humility.

NOTES

1. Quotations from *The Rule of St Benedict* (*RSB*) are taken from the translation by David Parry OSB (London: Darton, Longman, & Todd, 1984).

2. Al Gini, 'Moral Leadership and Business Ethics' in Joanne B Ciulla (ed.), *Ethics, the Heart of Leadership* (Praeger; Westport, CT, 2004).

3. John Donne, *Devotions*, p.17. The full quotation is: 'No man is an island, entire of itself; every man is a piece of the Continent, a part of the main.'

4. *Centesimus Annus,* an Encyclical Letter of Pope John Paul II, written in 1991 to mark the centenary of the first of the social encyclicals, *Rerum Novarum*, written by Pope Leo XIII in 1891.

5. Christopher Jamison OSB, *Finding Sanctuary—Monastic steps for everyday life* (Weidenfeld & Nicolson, 2006) has a very helpful chapter on humility.

6. This understanding is developed by Joanne Ciulla in her essay, 'Leadership Ethics: Mapping the Territory', in Joanne B Ciulla (ed.), *Ethics, the Heart of Leadership,* (Praeger, Westport, CT, 2004).

7. GIFT

— **Nick Fane & Andrew Lightbown** —

*This is how we know what love is: Jesus Christ laid
down his life for us. And we ought to lay down
our lives for our brothers. If anyone has material
possessions and sees his brother in need but has no
pity on him, how can the love of God be in him?*
I JOHN 3.16–18 (NIV)

*Selfishness makes people deaf and dumb; love
opens eyes and hearts, enabling people to make
that original and irreplaceable contribution
which, together with thousands of deeds of so
many brothers and sisters, often distant and
unknown, converges to form the mosaic of
charity which can change the tide of history.*
POPE JOHN PAUL II[1]

Charity has come to be devalued. It is seen as outdated, paternalistic
and patronising, clouded by shades of the workhouse. Yet we
believe, along with Pope John Paul II (quoted above) that this
old-fashioned theological virtue can change not just an individual's
immediate circumstances, but the entire shape of history. It is
time to rediscover its original sense of love for one's fellow men
and women—a prompting, intriguingly, which is neither entirely
rational nor fully explicable in terms of genetics or psychology,
and yet it is an impulse that can transform both the receiver and
the giver. Some of the views sketched out in this reflection are
taken from our earlier book *(Re-) Discovering Charity*, and we are
grateful to Quicken Trust for allowing us to tell the story of some
of the people they have invested in.

Put simply, in theonomic terms, charity is the giving of an asset—something of value—by one person to another out of love in order to improve the well-being (material or spiritual) of that other. If, on the other hand, we give away something of no value to us, something entirely surplus to our requirement, that is not charity—even if it may still be a very worthwhile thing to do. From the theonomic perspective, charity is concerned with the voluntary redistribution of valued assets rather than surplus, or even superfluous, ones. Let us pause and ask ourselves a simple question: Which are we most likely to value: a gift whose giver has made a personal sacrifice to part with it, or one (however pleasing) which has only been given because the giver did not want it?

The meaning of charity is love, the kind of love for which the New Testament used the Greek word *agape*, and which C.S. Lewis helpfully distinguished from three other Greek words for forms of love: *storge*, *philia*, and *eros*, which can be translated respectively as affection, friendship, and romance.[2] Lewis recognised that agape in particular released a life-giving force that was beyond the scope of reason, and that part of our purpose is to liberate its potential. As always, Lewis is spot on. The divine impulse towards charity has to be brought to life by our God-given free will. We have the potential to love others as God loves us, but the onus rests on us. *Agape* implies a radical form of giving of self, both materially and spiritually, for the benefit of another human being.

Sources differ as to the origin of the phrase 'Charity begins at home', but the earliest recorded English use is Wyclif's fourteenth century 'Charite schuld bigyne at hem-self'.[3] Although this interestingly echoes Jesus' commandment to 'love thy neighbour as thyself', with its implication that unless one is right with oneself one cannot properly give love to one's neighbour, we see it rather differently. We suggest that charity begins at home because that is where we are most easily hospitable—or, to put it another way, in the football league of life, *agape* is found in the hospitality of home games; charity is *agape* expressed in the away fixtures. We would argue that acting on a sense of *agape* is more than simply a spontaneous reaction to someone else's ill-being. It may be a rapid response to an event, but, crucially, is not instinctive. It is the conscious product of free will, in the exercise of which we may choose to listen to God. It is an action, moving in the direction of another person. Certainly that is how it was from Karl Barth's perspective, for he viewed *agape*, and indeed faith itself, not as inherent in human nature, but as the decided actions of particular individuals.[4]

The point is this, surely: we can choose to become one of those individuals, just as the Good Samaritan did. And, in this respect, Richard Dawkins is right to observe that only we humans, among all the creatures on earth, have the capacity to override the despotic selfishness of our biological drives.[5]

So, is charity an exclusively Christian virtue? Well, clearly the Good Samaritan was not a Christian,[6] and nor, for that matter, was Jesus. But that is to miss the central point, which is that there is an impulse towards charity which does not stem from our reason, nor from our biology, and which, we would argue, comes from God. It is an impulse to which we can be sensitised, and which can be reinforced, by a commitment to spiritual practice. But we simply cannot know all the possible ways that God—as Father, Son, and Holy Spirit—works in the world, nor through whom he works. So, we would suggest that our human impulse to be charitable is animated through Christ, even in those who do not acknowledge him. Perhaps less controversial is the theonomic perspective that sees charity as inescapably linked with justice. An economic system that is based entirely on 'What can I get?' fails to meet the principles of justice. We want to focus instead on the question 'What can I give?' (and, yes, we do recognise that I cannot give what I have not got!). As Kierkegaard reminds us, we are all absolutely equal before God.[7] Rabbi Jonathon Sacks adds another dimension by arguing that we need to rediscover the old religious traditions about human solidarity, justice, compassion and the ultimate dignity of the person.[8] Furthermore, as Rowan Williams has pointed out, 'to get the full sense of the parable of the Good Samaritan, we need to use another word: the good asylum seeker, the good Muslim, the good teenager in a hoodie.'[9] We like his formulation because you can insert your own prejudices and feel what it is like to love unconditionally those you despise.

The definition that we have developed to describe what we have called 'realised *agape*', in other words, *agape* in action, is: 'To act intentionally to promote well-being in solidarity with, and in reverential response to, others.'

Solidarity means, in this context, being fully alongside another person in their distress. Givers experience solidarity in one of two ways: sympathetically or empathetically. Sympathy means being cold to our own wants and desires in an effort to support an afflicted individual or group. When experiencing true sympathy, we reflect imaginatively on the life of the sufferer and contemplate how we would feel were we in the same position. Many people making donations to charities such as Quicken Trust are motivated by sympathy in the sense that we have described it. Empathy is somewhat different for it implies a more radical erosion of the border between the giver and the receiver. Empathy is associated with vocation or 'calling'. If in sympathy we attempt to feel what it is like to be in someone else's shoes, in empathy we imaginatively become the other—the same kind of difference that exists between simile and metaphor. Christian counsellors, such as those providing support for sufferers in Kabubbu, Uganda, as part of the Quicken Trust mission, experience a deep sense of empathy. The response is in both cases reverential in the sense of having unconditional regard for all human beings as uniquely created. Both of these meanings encompass justice and promote giving, or, as C.S Lewis called it, 'gift-love.'

Such depths of feeling are apparent in the parable of the Good Samaritan (Luke 10.25–37), in which Jesus answers a lawyer who asked him: 'Who is my neighbour?' Jesus tells of a man who, while on a journey, was attacked by robbers and left for dead. Two Jewish officials, fearing ritual contamination through contact with a corpse, pass him by on the other side of the road, but a Samaritan (a racial group whom the Jews despised) goes to his aid and pays for his care. The answer is that our neighbour is anyone in need. Human need, pure and simple, puts a claim on our love that transcends all the usual boundaries of race, class, religion or gender. Jesus tells the lawyer: 'Go and do likewise'—to love others, to take them to a place of safety, to ask others to help, and to promise to remain committed. But the story also suggests that none of this is possible unless the 'lover' is capable of being moved in his innermost being. One might also recall Jesus' own response on encountering a leper when, as St Mark relates, he was 'moved to anger'—a reaction experienced viscerally as well as emotionally, involving a physicality which is enacted when Jesus reaches out and touches the leper. (Mark 1.40–42) And, as Psalm 51 says, such ability to experience 'truth in the inward being', leading to the ability to reach out to others, can only flourish when a person has purged his or her mind of material considerations: 'Create in me a clean heart, O God, and put a new and right spirit within me.'

We are aware that there are those who would say that charity is no more than altruism, and that it is a well-established biological principle that altruism exists for good evolutionary reasons—either because it protects the family gene pool, or because if I scratch your back you might scratch mine! So why, asked John Polkinghorne in *Questions of Truth*, does a man save an unknown and unrelated person from a burning building?[10] Whose genes benefit? Does he expect to be rescued in return? Genetically, it seems to be an irrational act. And think of the Good Samaritan. Did he gain by his act in any way? Why on earth did he behave as he did? What is clear is that charity, just like hospitality, implies the willing acceptance of risk and the foregoing of return. The theonomic equation is asymmetrical.

Nor is it not the same as philanthropy. Philanthropy is a very good thing, and there are many who have good cause to thank philanthropists, from Andrew Carnegie, with his public libraries, to Bill Gates, with his polio and AIDS foundations. But philanthropy tends to be the preserve of the wealthy, whilst charity is the province of the many. Philanthropy usually promotes general or communal well-being. Charity is about individual giving and receiving, with the receiver often personally passing on the baton. Philanthropy is frequently conditional, in that it is given in the expectation of recognition. Another distinction is that philanthropy is a top down, macro solution, whereas charity and hospitality are bottom up, incarnational and direct. Furthermore, *agape*-love, of which charity and hospitality are expressions, tends to follow the scriptural stricture to give in private.[11]

The fact that charitable giving is often anonymous, or at least below the radar, provides a serious challenge to economic theory that has, for various reasons, sought to become increasingly precise and scientific. Modern economics devotes a great deal of time counting, quantifying, and producing reams of statistics, often presented in comparative forms, such as league tables. In reality are we not deeply suspicious of such approaches? Are not some courses of action simply worthwhile, good or virtuous in their own right? Perhaps the fact that true virtue is beyond measurement is the real splendour in what economists since Adam Smith have referred to as the 'invisible hand'. And it goes without saying that charity is not the same as aid, which usually comes with political or ideological strings that are in the interests of the giver not the receiver. Another distinction can be made between charity and alms-giving. The latter is a duty, a responsibility, whereas charity and hospitality go beyond duty.

We have also come to see a distinction between realised *agape* and vocational *agape*. Enhanced well-being is a consequence of improvements in a person's economic, social, psychological, and spiritual standing. *Agape* does not lend or subsidise: it gives. And it does so unconditionally: in *agape* there are no limited liabilities. Realised *agape* always gives both materially and spiritually, and is not reducible to either straightforward giving or to emotion. Vocational *agape*, the result of a sense or awareness of calling, can involve giving physically, psychologically, and spiritually (for example, the nineteenth century priests who gave their health and, ultimately, their lives to succour cholera victims). With both of these forms of *agape*, there is an element of personal relationship, and a giving which exacts a, sometimes highly significant, personal opportunity cost.

So how can we tell charity if we see it? The truth is that we may never see it at all. For, as we have already suggested, giving is often done anonymously, yet its effects are manifest. Think of the three Rs: charity is Reverent, Responsible and Radical; it is not Rational, Reciprocal or Restrictive.

Not all objections to charity are insubstantial. Mohammed Yunus, the eminent economist, business man, and Nobel prize-winner, has challengingly questioned not people's inbuilt desire to help others through charity, nor their sense of duty, but the manner in which charity is often dispensed. He believes that charity can have highly damaging effects on those who receive it, stripping away both their dignity and their incentive to strive for themselves. He suggests it leads to passivity and complacency about relying on others.[12]

Although Yunus' point appears to echo the frequently made charge that charity creates dependency, he almost certainly has in mind the kind of institutionalised charity that comes with an agenda and conditions. However, we think it is a far weaker point when applied to the individual unconditional giving of one to another which *agape* describes. We are all dependent on someone, and, we would argue, ultimately upon God. Why is that wrong? Is it always wrong for me to depend on others, and for others to depend on me? In the stories of the people of Kabubbu that we told in our book, *(Re)-Discovering Charity)*[13] we found plenty of evidence on the ground to challenge the notion that *agape* creates passivity and robs people of dignity. Our evidence is that Christian charity fosters responsibility.

There is also an important difference between *charity* and *charities*. Charities, from a theonomic perspective, can be seen as institutional agents of virtue, sitting between the donor and the recipient. Without such virtue, charities are really nothing more than hollow institutional structures. Charities vary enormously in size and nature, from quasi-governmental organizations to small voluntary groups. Many charities provide a way in which individuals can pursue their own agency, often in a small way. Indeed it is often the small achievable things that count for most in the real world. Dietrich Bonhoeffer has reminded us that it is not for us to try to change the whole world, but simply to do what needs to be done, realistically, in particular circumstances.[14] For example, it would be unrealistic (not to say simply silly) for an individual wishing to donate £50 to benefit a child in Uganda to spend £500 on a plane ticket so as to be able to deliver the gift personally. Individual charity, though, certainly can happen through direct action, as the parable of the Good Samaritan—Jesus' answers the lawyer's (and our) fundamental question—illustrates. With great succinctness, Bishop Gene Robinson answers this same question, 'What must I do?', by saying we must love in a way that hurts, that costs us something, whether that be time, money, or convenience.[15] Without experiencing such love for our neighbour, we can never experience 'eternal life'.

In our grounded research in Uganda we came across many examples of the effect of *agape* expressed in direct action. Let us take as an example Rose, who had received, through the institutional agency of Quicken Trust, the gift of a house from funds provided by an individual donor in the UK. Rose's first baby had been delivered in the bush during the civil war, and had died, and over the years the violence had exhausted her. Her family of ten had previously lived in a single room. This is what Rose says now: 'It's been like a miracle, a gift from God. A surprise, just a wonderful surprise. An achievement we never dreamt about. A wonder. I have no words to express it.' Far from creating a crippling reliance on external support, the freely given gift has been freely accepted, and it has enabled Rose to be an effective mother of her children, in turn providing them with the opportunity to grow into effective, loving adults themselves.

Agnes tells a similar story. Her children had been brought up in a local banana-beer bar, in daily sight and earshot of drunkenness and lechery, but now, through charity, they are re-housed. This is what Agnes says: 'My situation is very different now. I have hope. There was a time when I had even lost the desire to have a nice home. Now I feel a challenge and a sense of responsibility, something I had never dreamt of. It has made me more ambitious and encouraged me to work. My daughter has become more loving. Before, I believed God had forgotten about me. Now I'm thankful, and at times I think that even if I don't pray, God still knows about me. But I do pray.' Agnes had been desperately worried that her daughter would be seduced from her dark and cramped back room at the pub by the lure of drugs and prostitution. Now both mother and daughter have rediscovered the relationship that had nearly foundered, and the prospect of a stable future is much increased. Interest on an investment indeed.

And, finally, Prosy, who lives with two of her children and six grandchildren, for whom she has cared alone, since the untimely and distressing death of her best friend, her husband. At first she did this by growing food on a small plot of 'common' land, which was suddenly confiscated. She became isolated and desperate. Then she was given a hen-house and thirty chickens. Through her industry and determination, she has now been transformed from subsistence farmer to village expert on poultry husbandry; she is respected and admired. She is now able to say: 'A mother always feels happy and becomes a good mother when she has something to give her family, especially when she is recovering from a situation when there was nothing at all to put on the table. What has happened has eased my loneliness and I now feel very self-sustaining. It has helped remove that feeling of losing a friend and having to stand alone.'

These do not sound like people whom charity has robbed of dignity, who have been disincentivised to work, who are sticking out their hands believing the world owes them a living.

Hospitality—*agape* at home—sounds nice and safe, even cosy: 'More tea, Vicar?' Yet something that happened close to us in quiet Buckingham—definitely home rather than away—shows the true face of hospitality. Ron and Mary live in an old but elegant house in a pleasant road close to the town centre. They are now retired, but, not so many years ago, Ron was still working as a teacher and Mary as a nurse, and they had a family of three. One very cold winter evening, the children long in bed, while taking the dogs out for their evening breath of air, Ron went across to a nearby waste patch. He had not gone far, only as far as the phone box at the end of the road in fact, when he noticed a young man huddled on the floor of the kiosk, hands around his drawn-up knees in an attempt to compress himself enough to close the door.

Many of us at this point would have slightly quickened our pace, and suddenly noticed something interesting on the other side of the road. But Ron didn't. He wished he that he could pass by, but instead he went to warn and consult Mary. She couldn't ignore the situation either. So he did something most of us would consider unwise, reckless, or even potentially dangerous. He went over to the box, opened the door, and actually spoke to the young man. He initiated a conversation, and persuaded the young man to follow him back across the road and inside. They discovered through the young man's accent that he was originally from Glasgow, had been turned out by his parents a year before, found his way to Buckingham, and then realised he had nowhere to go and no money to buy fares or food. He did not want to beg, or ask for help, but he realised he needed shelter for the night, and then tomorrow would bring what it would bring. So he had taken refuge in the small red glasshouse provided by BT with his only possessions, including a pipe for making music.

Mary gave him food and tea and they chatted—with difficulty, since his Glaswegian accent was very thick. They established that he had left home and was just wandering. He eventually expressed a wish for a guitar, and, being lent one, he played it and sang. What he sang was unintelligible to Ron and Mary, but there was no doubt his whole soul was in the music he played. He slept in a sleeping bag in front of the fire, with the dogs in the passage. Mary and Ron and their three children slept upstairs in their usual rooms. The young man could have harmed or even killed any one or all of them in the night. But he didn't. He could have stolen any of their property, food or money, and made off at dawn before they were awake. But he didn't. The next day he was given breakfast, and, after giving his thanks, he left. They tried to point him in the direction of the labour exchange, but, at around four o'clock, he was seen on the London road, thumbing a lift. Since he had forgotten his music pipe, Jackie, the youngest, begged to be allowed to take it to him, which she did.

He has not been heard of by the couple again, but they once gave a talk to their local church about their experience. They called it 'Entertaining Angels Unawares.' Of course we are in the sphere of metaphor here, but, as Lucy Winkett has astutely pointed out, to love an angel could be far more important that to believe in him.[16] And that love, that reckless love, what St Paul called agape, is what Ron and Mary gave to the stranger though their hospitality.

We would offer these final observations. First, if we are Christians, to act in charity is what we have been commanded to do, how we have been commanded to be. It is frighteningly simple. But the message beats like a drum throughout the gospels. Feed the hungry, care for the sick, welcome the stranger; whoever they are, wherever they come from, and whatever they have done. That is what Jesus did, that is what Love did, and does. 'For when I was hungry, you gave me food; when thirsty, you gave me drink; when I was a stranger you took me into your home.' (Matthew 25.35)

At home, then, charity is there in the hospitality, in its broadest sense, we may offer, if we choose, to those with whom we come into daily contact. Further afield, it is the support—whether financial, practical, or spiritual—we can give freely, if we choose, to those who need it. All such acts are vital threads in the tapestry of human flourishing.

SUMMARY

- *Agape* is the Greek word for the type of love that implies giving of oneself both materially and spiritually and as such goes beyond duty.
- Charity and hospitality are both manifestations of *agape*.
- Charity takes place away from home; hospitality takes place in the home or in an environment under the giver's control.

- In both charity and hospitality, it is the needs of the sufferer that are paramount.
- Any returns achieved as a result of the giving accrue to the recipient of what CS Lewis described as 'gift-love.'
- Givers willingly accept risk. The relationship is therefore asymmetrical.
- Charity and hospitality are both bottom-up, incarnational strategies.
- Giving is frequently anonymous.
- Charities, when viewed through the theonomic lens, can be regarded as agents of virtue.

NOTES

1. Pope John II, 'Message to Youth', World Youth Day, 26 November, 1995.
2. C S Lewis, *The Four Loves* (Harvest Books, 1960).
3. John Wyclif, *English Works* (c.1383). This saying was first expressed as we now understand it by Sir Thomas Browne, *Religio Medici*, 1642: 'But how shall we expect charity towards others, when we are so uncharitable to ourselves? 'Charity begins at home', is the voice of the world; yet is every man his greatest enemy, and, as it were, his own executioner.'
4. Karl Barth *Church Dogmatics* (T&T Clark; Edinburgh, 1961).
5. Richard Dawkins, *The Selfish Gene* (OUP: Oxford, 1989).
6. The Parable of the Good Samaritan (Luke 10.25–37).
7. Søren Kierkegaard, *Preface to Two Discourses at the Communion on Friday,* cited in A Lightbown and N Fane, *(Re)Discovering Charity,* (University of Buckingham Press, 2009), p. 16.
8. Jonathan Sacks, *The Dignity of Difference* (Continuum, 2003). Copyright © Jonathan Sacks. Reproduced with permission of Continuum, an imprint of Bloomsbury Publishing Plc.
9. Rowan Williams, 'The Conflict Between Religion and Modernity' in *emel magazine* (1/12/2007).

GIFT **93**

10. John Polkinghorne, *Questions of Truth* (Westminster: John Knox, 2009).

11. Giving in secret is commended by Jesus in the Sermon on the Mount: 'Be careful not to parade your religion before others; if you do, no reward awaits you with your Father in heaven. So, when you give alms, do not announce it with a flourish of trumpets, as the hypocrites do . . . But when you give alms, do not let your left hand know what your right is doing; your good deed must be secret, and your Father who sees what is done in secret will reward you.' (Matthew 6.1–4)

12. Mohammed Yunus, *Banker to the Poor* (Aurum, 2009).

13. A. Lightbown and N. Fane, *(Re) Discovering Charity* (University of Buckingham Press, 2010).

14. Dietrich Bonhoeffer, cited in *Singing the Ethos of God* (Eerdmans publishing, 2007) Michigan, p. 90.

15. Gene Robinson, *In the Eye of the Storm* (Seabury Books, 2008).

16. Lucy Winkett, *Our Sound is Our Wound* (Continuum, 2010).

8.   A PRINCIPLED WAY TO INVEST

— **Frank Canosa** —

*The decision to invest is always
an ethical or moral one.*
JOHN PAUL II, *CENTESIMUS ANNUS*

The practice of investing in accordance with a set of values has a long pedigree. Seen from the Christian perspective, the concern for the welfare of one's fellow man that underpins the philosophy can be repeatedly found in the gospels. St Augustine of Hippo, in the fifth century, defined the distinction between a Christian and a pagan outlook to earthly life in his *De Civitate Dei contra Paganos*, normally known as *The City of God*. Many other learned Christian men and women throughout the centuries have written of their belief that the followers of Christ must operate under higher guiding principles. I can think readily of St. Benedict and St. Thomas Aquinas, although few have described a theocentric existence with greater passion and eloquence than St Teresa of Avila. These great thinkers were part of the historical thread that led to what is known today as Roman Catholic Social Teaching, a set of principles that are expected to guide a Catholic's place in society and his obligation to others. This theme of social responsibility has been a consistent preoccupation of papal encyclicals since Leo XIII's seminal *Rerum Novarum* in 1891.

John Wesley, in his famous sermon entitled 'The Use of Money' (1744), spoke of the need for man's activities to refrain from any harm to his neighbour. That subdivision of responsible investment that is today known as 'green investing' finds its root in Wesley's revulsion at the serious environmental effects of the tanning industry, although Wesley's concerns were specifically directed to the effects on the health of those involved. Wesley similarly spoke in the same sermon about anything that would encourage a lack of chastity in one's neighbour, thus underpinning today's negative screening of companies involved in pornography. The legacy of his influence is far from surprising. Wesley spoke and wrote within that astonishing period of human history that came to be known as the Age of Enlightenment, the remarkable eighteenth century after the birth of Christ. More than two centuries later, we are still marked by the patterns of both rational endeavour and social conscience that were so robustly postulated at the time.

Philosophically, Wesley and others neatly tie a sense of responsibility to the general welfare with investment. The disconnection is, in fact, illogical. A contemporary of Wesley who shared his aversion to the chemicals used in the tanning industry because of their noxious effect on the health of workers would have been inconsistent (and highly hypocritical) had he nevertheless invested in that industry. Ultimately, and in order to avoid contradiction, adherence to principle is as intrinsic a part of investment as it is to any other human endeavour.

It should also be stated, and especially in the context of investment, that Wesley was neither ashamed nor alarmed by the natural human instinct to make money. He firmly encouraged making the maximum profits from what he called 'honest industry'. That sense of 'honest industry' is revealed today in companies whose share price is supported by that consistency of profitability that follows from sound governance based on social responsibility. Furthermore, it can be postulated that dishonest endeavour leads to disaster. Corporate failure often comes from neither market conditions nor competitive pressures, but from the suspension of ethics and moral judgment. Union Carbide, WorldCom, and Enron are but the more notable examples. More recently, great names in the world of finance have become relegated to history from having succumbed to an ethos of irresponsible greed that became part of their corporate fabric. Excess was the reason for their demise, not the corporate imperative to make money. The imperative itself was perverted into an irresponsible hunt for short term profits or competitive advantage with little thought for long term risk. The long-term depression in the market price of bank shares is evidence of the injury that was made to shareholders. A company's failure to pursue 'honest industry' leads, sooner or later, to serious economic loss.

The persistent finding that honest industry leads to profitability is itself a bulwark for responsible investment. When I was a young banker actively involved in corporate finance, I was often struck by the correlation that exists between a corporate sense of civic and environmental responsibility and shareholder value. This economic rationale is one that has been eloquently embodied in the principles behind many corporate pension schemes, including that of the British Broadcasting Company (BBC). I attended a conference on socially responsible investing many years ago with one of the trustees. He told me of his strong belief, shared by the other trustees, that companies with sound governance and a preoccupation with the interests of the wider stakeholder would invariably render better performance and, therefore, a higher return to investors.

The terminology used in this more selective type of investment is sometimes confusing, even to practitioners. Many believe that the terms responsible investment, socially responsible investment, and ethical investment are synonymous. They are not, and each represents a narrowing of the investable universe over the previous one. I shall endeavour to give my own definitions, but with the warning that many colleagues in the financial services industry may disagree. The terms arise from generally accepted opinion rather than from an established lexicon. I justify my definitions for their being rationally derived and empirically useful. They have provided the means for common parlance with clients, and have therefore produced a thorough mutual understanding of investment intentions.

Responsible Investment is the broadest of the categories and encompasses the largest number of potential investments. Responsible investment should be the basis for all decisions as it is based on an exhaustive scrutiny of a given company's prospects based on a full quantitative and qualitative analysis. All elements should be taken into account. These should include the attraction of the company's product to the market, its competitive position, the soundness of its financial statements and financial ratios, and the commercial acumen, probity and calibre of its management. So indeed will the diligence and trustworthiness of its corporate governance structures and internal procedures. This last aspect is very important in the context of responsible investment. The world's leading producer of widgets with a positive tick mark against all of the above would fail to qualify as responsible investment if it obtained contracts through bribery. This need not arise from a moral aversion to bribery, but merely from a cool assessment of the repercussions. These might, for instance, include detriment to the company's competitive standing, and the regulatory and judicial costs that would ensue, all of which would be strongly detrimental to its financial results. Similarly, responsible investment makes no moral assessment as to the company's product as long as its manufacture and distribution fall, of course, within legal and regulatory constraints. On a similar basis, responsible investing generally excludes companies whose processes may have a detrimental effect on the environment or on the health of its workers or wider stakeholders. Again, this is based on the recognition that such companies are likely to fall foul of government standards and become subject to fines or civil lawsuits. Both consequences would of course be damaging to investment performance. Responsible investment is therefore concerned with the financial consequences of corporate misdeeds rather than the repugnance that may arise from a moral stand. As such, it admittedly has the flimsiest ethical foundations of the categories that we are discussing, even if its objectives are shared with those whose investments reflect a set of values.

Socially Responsible Investing, or 'SRI', represents a considerable narrowing of the investable universe. It is the first of our categories that is based on moral principle. Normally, companies that are involved in the production of tobacco, armaments, pornography, alcohol and gambling are excluded from investment under the concept of SRI. These prohibitions are so universal that they have become known as 'the five exclusions'. They arise from investor reluctance to become involved in companies whose products directly engender the ill health or death of humans (tobacco, alcohol, armaments), or that cater to our baser instincts and are therefore deleterious to human dignity (pornography, gambling). The general acceptance today of the five exclusions has allowed investment houses to issue funds for wide distribution to retail investors that are based on these principles. The process of exclusion of companies involved in these prohibited sectors is known as 'negative screening'.

Ethical Investing represents specific and individual moral values that arise from principle or faith. Although ethical constraints are generally dictated by the investor, companies have been known to take a specific ethical stance. For instance, Anita Roddick took the decision to eschew animal testing and foster fair trade when launching The Body Shop. Many may argue that such corporate initiatives are powerful marketing ploys at a time of heightened sensitivity. Indeed, when The Body Shop was launched, there was increasing public concern about the cruel frivolity of testing cosmetics on helpless animals. Nevertheless, I favour applause over cynicism, since such corporate initiatives establish markers towards a more caring society. Wesley, who favoured the gaining of all one can from honest industry, would have approved.

The ethical investor may hold beliefs that, even if shared by many, may nevertheless prove to be too exclusive to provide economic justification for the launch of a fund. Some ethical investors are unable to find refuge in the broader spectrum of SRI since their ethical stand may not be fully reflected within the five exclusions. The investment demand of some ethical investors may even be unsatisfied by the standard SRI exclusions because the exclusions are themselves unacceptable. For instance, a Roman Catholic investor may choose not to invest in pharmaceuticals engaged in stem cell research but would be content with alcohol producers, a standard SRI exclusion. Some ethical investors see the SRI exclusion of tobacco and gambling as demeaning to God-given free will and injurious to the self-restraint that should form part of man's moral fibre. The multiplicity of principle attendant on ethical investment therefore brings problems to a financial services industry where cost control is a function of volume.

Professional investment managers are generally able to keep their fees at a reasonable level by adapting their clients' investment parameters to a limited number of portfolio models that adapt to the expectations of most of their clients. These models vary depending on the client's acceptance of risk and the need either to derive income, or to plough it in for the sake of growth. Very specific ethical considerations fall outside models. Clients with unusual ethical demands will therefore need to meet a minimum threshold for investment, generally in the millions of pounds, in order to justify the additional costs that the managers must incur from the additional oversight and screening that is required. The screening can generally be outsourced, and there are a number of companies that undertake it, of which the best known is EIRIS (Experts in Responsible Investment Solutions), set up thirty years ago. Nevertheless, all screening bears a cost regardless of whether it is internal to the portfolio manager or outsourced. Therefore a totally bespoke investment service is available to few, and investment in accordance with individual moral preferences, whether inspired by religion or not, remains elusive for most.

Ethical investment is, therefore, often undertaken by individual investors making their own informed choices. Where the ethical investor is of sufficient wealth to justify the costs of a tailored ethical portfolio, the investment manager needs to follow a number of steps. As is appropriate with the planned composition of all investment portfolios, the process starts with a clear-headed assessment of the level of risk that the client wishes to assume. Acceptable risk, which in portfolio management refers more to the volatility of an investment than to an outright risk of loss, informs the proportion among asset classes. These asset classes include equities, bonds, cash and a span of alternative investments. The factors that have to be considered in determining the appropriate relation of risk to return are complex, and they depend on the many elements that pertain to the client's life circumstances. These are viewed against the traditional volatilities of the particular asset classes, and are reliant on prevailing and expected market conditions.

Once these parameters have been established, the client can then proceed to focus on how ethics should affect investment decisions. The terms of reference vary depending on the client's moral compass and desired exclusions. The ethical guidelines that result create the blueprint to which the investment manager adheres. The guidelines sometimes allow flexibility as to the level as well as the nature of involvement in certain proscribed activities. For example, computer software is present in weapon technology, but it would not make sense to ban software producers from investment since the total profitability that most such companies derive from weapon applications is comparatively small. Furthermore, most investors acknowledge the need for democracies to maintain a robust defence industry. The line would be drawn, of course, were a given software producer to grant licences to rogue states or even inadequately to police access by those who would use its products for malevolent purposes. This sensible rationale also curtails blame on companies whose otherwise innocuous products are used for evil. Mobile telephony was used to trigger the Madrid bombings, but blame can hardly be apportioned to the manufacturers of the telephones. As in most moral judgments, the exercise of free will provides guidance. Therefore, a media company that ventures into pornography will be deemed to have crossed the line regardless of how limited its involvement in this proscribed area might be.

Ethical investment guidelines should apply to all asset classes even if their operation is more often seen in the purchase of corporate equities and bonds. There is a general rule, for instance, against making deposits in banks that have dealings with dictatorships or any government that exploits its people. This is sometimes difficult to determine since the legitimate good served by banking secrecy has the flip side of obscuring a bank's dealings with unsavoury individuals and governments. As a result, ethical guidelines generally accept that this proscription can operate only through the notoriety that comes from adverse publicity. Ethical restrictions on bank deposits have a fine tradition, and have been used to dissuade banks from lending or financing trade with certain regimes, such as South Africa during apartheid and

Pinochet's Chile. The venerable Riggs Bank of Washington D.C., which had flourished for over a century and a half, ceased to exist in 2005 after being brought down by a series of scandals involving money laundering and covert relationships with foreign dictators. Deposits are a key component to bank profitability since they are the primary means for funding the loan base. A bank that strays can therefore be castigated by investors who will pull or withhold deposits, as well as avoid the bank's shares and bond issues, creating a veritable 'triple whammy'.

Although ethical investment guidelines have traditionally focused on proscriptions and areas to avoid, there is greater emphasis today on rewarding the managers of companies who seek to benefit the environment and their fellow man. Many clients, as well as pension schemes, instruct those who manage their investments to purchase the securities of companies that have assiduously pursued a socially responsible charter, or that have made an outstanding contribution to the improvement of human life or to the environment. This positive, rather than negative, screening is increasingly being enthusiastically endorsed by investors who wish to sponsor those companies that have shown distinction in working towards our common welfare. The case for either negative or positive screening as a determinant of financial performance may be largely neutral. In other words, whether the guidelines screen out the worst or highlight the best performers as to social responsibility, the net result is a choice from among those companies that have a social conscience and provide higher economic benefits. Nevertheless, since it acknowledges and rewards the best performers, positive screening may have a greater effect in encouraging companies to excel. What is known today as 'impact investing' goes beyond positive screening. Impact investors invest in companies that have societal and/or environmental benefit as the primary objective, with profit and other considerations being secondary. There is, therefore, a strong philanthropic component to impact investing since return on investment and investment performance become secondary motivations.

Other than in impact investing, most investors today see superior financial performance is the commercial underpinning of SRI and much ethical investment. In fact, the empirical evidence for this is so overwhelming that the economic rationale behind SRI is today generally accepted. As a Visiting Professor at EDHEC, the French business school, I have often been asked to be the thesis advisor by students who wish to explore some variation on this theme, i.e., that higher financial returns are produced by companies that abide by their responsibilities to the stakeholder. More gratifying is the fact that moral grounds that exclude the profit motive are instinctively accepted by the new generation. It is pertinent, especially in the context of this book, to explore how moral values underlie a motivation that is separate from the search for profit.

There can be, of course, a purely secular footing to both SRI and ethical investing. The human moral compass may have been enhanced by religion and inspired by it, but it is not solely dependent on faith. Humanist philosophy will, by itself, guide an atheist to a socially responsible investment policy, and even into a distinct ethical line. Investors who reject animal testing, or companies that exploit the looser regulatory directives of the Third World, or who refuse to invest in nuclear power because of the potential environmental effects, are taking distinct ethical positions that go beyond SRI. There is no reason why these principled decisions should not be taken by an atheist.

The need to embrace a broad Church (or the absence of one) becomes especially relevant when investing on behalf of disparate persons. Ethical investment becomes somewhat complicated when it is espoused by a group, be it a body corporate, a charity, or any other association of individuals. They are not investing their own money but the money of others. The representatives of the group (be they trustees, a board, or a management committee) respond to the desires of those for whom they act. They are mere stewards of the money. There is a time-hallowed, and legally protected, fiduciary duty that compels the trustee to act exclusively in the interests of those on whose behalf the trustee holds control of the funds. Modern corporate governance places a similar responsibility on a company's board and management. In a secular corporation, those interests are, of course, primarily financial, but they also should reflect the beliefs of those to whom the fiduciary duty is owed. In this way, a pension scheme might not only seek the highest financial return within the confines of prudence, but may seek to do so while reflecting the liberal humanist values of its employees. This, of course, does not mean that all employees need necessarily subscribe to a pension fund's SRI or ethical constraints. Some without religion will nevertheless feel themselves attuned to tenets that seek the greater good. Those unmoved by a moral imperative will perceive the SRI, and perhaps the ethical agenda, as a key component to an enhanced financial return. The goal is articulated through the premise that only those companies that follow a socially responsible system of governance will provide the pension holders with higher levels of sustained performance. The motivation for some may, therefore, remain financial, whereas others within the group will find satisfaction in the moral component.

True morally inspired investment guidelines generally remain within the sphere of charities, religious organizations and individuals. As we have noted with impact investing, principle may govern even to the possible impairment of financial return. By way of example, an abhorrence of embryonic stem cell research may be detrimental to portfolio returns. It may lead to the avoidance of pharmaceutical companies that represent good defensive holdings in a declining economy, or biotechnology companies that have significant growth prospects. A refusal to invest in alcohol producers bars a significant number of luxury goods conglomerates that show excellent returns during a rising curve in the economic cycle. The trustees who take responsibility for investing ethically at the risk of financial sacrifice have to obtain consensus from the members or subscribers of funds. This is generally not a problem for smaller charities or religious communities with a common vocation and strongly shared values. Striking a balance becomes difficult, however, for trustees of charities that may be founded on religious grounds but whose activities rely on a wide base of contributors who seek the financial returns that will more robustly serve the cause. I was once closely involved with a religious charity that squared the circle by not contemplating any long term investment at all, but opted rather to distribute contributions as soon as possible, and certainly within a year's time horizon. In this way, its investments remained ethically neutral and of brief duration, and were restricted to short-term deposits with major banks and short-dated Government securities. Although, as we have seen, banks sometimes stray into morally contentious territory, deposits of short duration allowed this charity to make an early reassessment of existing positions in case that wrongful action on the part of the bank came to light.

The field is evolving. Responsible investment is largely the norm among investment managers and the serious investor today. Socially responsible investment has made its mark, and there is a proliferation of funds, some of which even go beyond the traditional five exclusions and therefore become borderline with ethical investment. Although ethical investment remains an area of considerable divergence in investor intentions, a number of funds have appeared that cater to individual religious groups. The environmental focus of green investing, and the philanthropic and progressive aims of impact investing strategies, create additional diversity within the sector. We should celebrate the fact that the moral threshold continues to shift. Investment indices such as FTSE4Good indicate that modern investment has an additional dimension.

Is this reflective of a more profound ethical dimension to human endeavour? One likes to think so. I have stated my firm belief that the humanist approach is sufficient for an investor to approach investment from a socially responsible or even an ethical outlook. However, there is much in both types of investment that responds to Christian principles. I am particularly struck by the echo of Roman Catholic Social Teaching that I hear so clearly in SRI and ethical investment guidelines. The five exclusions of SRI are aligned to Social Teaching in sponsoring respect for the dignity of the individual, safeguarding the life and health of others and the call for solidarity as one human family. Most significantly, perhaps,

Social Teaching espouses the notion that we are all stewards of Creation. That, I believe, has special resonance within socially responsible and ethical investment theory and practice.

We have discussed and seen this concept of stewardship in the role of trustees of charities, pensions and those who are responsible for corporate investment. They are the mere stewards of the wealth that has been placed in their care. I would like to posit, however, that all wealth, whether corporate or individual, demands stewardship. If so, the responsibility that comes with stewardship calls for an ethical code when investing.

It is easy enough for those who inherit wealth to think in this way. That which they possess is but a happy accident of birth. Even their natural selfish desire will lead them to preserve the wealth for the benefit of their children. When all is said and done, they are stewards of wealth. Their husbandry of that gift will therefore be cautious and never wasteful. It will have that strong instinct for indefinite preservation that is both the hallmark of stewardship and of our obligation to our fellow creatures and their environment. The instinct to preserve is the closest we can come to eternity, and for Christians, eternity is our stock in trade.

But what of the self-made man, he who has pulled himself up from nothing and who owes his wealth merely to his own labour? Surely, there is no nature of gift here but merely a case of wealth as the reward for effort. Further reflection, however, shows the fallacy of such thinking. Any successful entrepreneur will admit the inescapable fact that many others will have laboured harder and yet failed. Many a self-made man will accept that his wealth has come from a happy mixture of talent and luck. Both talent and luck are beyond striving. They are a gift and a godsend. And justice demands that a gift from Providence be employed for the good of Creation.

> By God's grace I am what I am, and his grace to me has
> not proved in vain; in my labours I have out-done them
> all—not I, indeed, but the grace of God working with me.
> *1 Corinthians 15.10*

9. WORK

— Nick Bion —

*The purpose of a business firm is not simply
to make a profit, but is to be found in its very
existence as a community of persons who
in various ways are endeavouring to satisfy
their basic needs, and who form a particular
group at the service of the whole of society.*
POPE JOHN PAUL II, *CENTESIMUS ANNUS*

In *90,000 Hours*, Rodney Green asks whether jobs exist in a spiritual hierarchy, with missionaries and vicars at the top, doctors and teachers a little lower down, and ordinary jobs in industry, commerce and government at the bottom.[1] It is a question that may well have occurred to others who have decided to give 90,000 hours of their life to secular employment. It is a question for others to answer. In this chapter we examine what a Christian may do in such secular employment.

In Britain today, we live in a society which places little value on ownership of businesses. It is often said that it does not matter who owns the companies but where the jobs are. Companies are seen as existing to provide financial returns for shareholders. For public companies, a system of stock market share ownership devolves the responsibilities of the shareholders' ownership to directors of companies whose only remit to the owners is to maximise shareholder value, being understood in terms of share value and dividends. By contrast, a private company can allow for wider responsibilities of ownership: to customers, suppliers, employees, the environment and its community. I run a specialist sheet metal processing business: How do I approach these other responsibilities?

I do not see the company existing solely for my benefit and that of other shareholders. As the majority shareholder, I hold the company in trust during my tenure, just as the owner of a piece of land or a famous painting may consider themselves to be holding it in trust for others. Buying a famous painting may give you the right to burn it, but this does not make it the right thing to do.

When I first started running the business I met many times with financial advisers and accountants who assumed that my aim would be to build up the business and sell it for as much as I could get. At present, British society appears to support this with generous tax treatment of capital gains, as the profits from selling a business are taxed at about a quarter of the rate of employment in a business. It was also assumed that I would want to pay as little tax as possible. Paying as little tax as possible is set up by the media as a noble goal rather than a shirking of one's responsibilities. It is quite clear that, as Christians, we should pay tax; as St Paul says in his letter to the Romans, 'if you owe taxes, pay taxes'. (Romans 13. 7, NIV) Without tax, for us, there would be no state schools or hospitals.

The first responsibility must be to run a successful and profitable company; without this one will find it very difficult to exercise any other responsibility.

Our responsibilities to customers are to honour the contracts, both written and implied, that we have entered into with them. It is not to mislead them, or allow them to commit to things that are not in their interests, nor to defraud or to cheat them. The prophet Amos, for example, condemns short measure, overcharging, tampering with the scales, and selling 'the refuse of the wheat'. (Amos 8.4–6) It is also not to exploit any situation our customers may find themselves in, but simply to provide excellent service and to charge a price commensurate with that service. It is also important that we do not do the customer's work at a loss or we may not be there to serve him in future, or even carry out the work he has given us. We also expect our customers to honour their part of the bargain. By the very nature of the market we are in, we can view all of our customers as long-term partners. Nothing is expected to be a one-off transaction, so the long term is everything. Orders from our customers are basic, and legal involvement is generally unknown. The contrast with purchasing our factory building could not be more marked. Purchase of property is essentially a one-off transaction with people you will never deal with again. There is no trust, no expectation that anything over what is legally required will be done. As a result, the legal work took over a month, and provided a file ten centimetres thick.

Our responsibilities to our suppliers mirror what we expect from our customers. We expect our suppliers to carry out the commitments they have made, and we must ensure that we carry out ours, namely to make clear what is required and to pay them on time. It is also good not to allow your suppliers to overcommit or to enter into something they do not understand. In practice you will find that many will seek to renegotiate a contract they do not see as fair. We also have a duty to stay in business. To go out of business, leaving your suppliers out of pocket, is to steal from your suppliers by deception: they have entered into an understanding with you, that if they carry out your order you will pay them. This may not be a fashionable view now, but it is nothing new from a religious perspective. Bankruptcy was not tolerated by the Religious Society of Friends: Joseph Fry, an unsuccessful banker, was disowned for not paying his creditors in 1829, though he was later re-instated 'with much admonition.'[2] During my time, I have come across more than one business that has been restarted after bankruptcy and has managed to pay off its previous creditors.

The company's responsibilities to its employees are to provide a safe place to work, treat them as ends in themselves and not only as a means to production, encourage them to act as partners in the business, and to support them during times of difficulty. We also have an obligation to reward fairly.

What is a fair rate of pay? On this subject the Church is largely silent. There are injunctions not to grind the faces of the poor, but what then? In the end, our view is that we should pay the market rate for the job. The worker deserves his pay. We should not pay somebody less because they like working in the company and would not leave, nor should we pay somebody too much so that they would not be able to find work elsewhere at a similar rate. The parable of the Workers in the Vineyard (Matthew 20.1–15) suggests that pay does not need to be equal, but the large pay differentials in our society may provide a challenge to our view of fairness.[3] Yet this is not something we can do much about since we must operate in the environment we are in. We do, however, operate a profit-related pay scheme for all employees which is worth about 20% of employees' salary. This is one way by which we provide 'effective participation in the whole production process, independently of the nature of services provided by the worker', and ensure that 'labour is not opposed to capital or capital to labour', as required by Catholic social teaching.[4]

For twenty years or more the company has observed the Sabbath. Our basis for this is the Ten Commandments, and is a question of sovereignty. By getting off the merry-go-round once a week, it has, for me, brought a sense of perspective to the business and, in the past, to other things that I regarded as my work. To know that there are other things that are more important than business, and that the business has to stop while other things are acknowledged, puts things in their proper place. It has also provided all our employees well defined periods of rest. We do work nights, but the 24/7 culture has not been one for us, although, with high capital investment in the business, a simplistic analysis would show that it should be beneficial. With society moving away from the need to keep Sunday as a day of rest for the majority of the population, we are under pressure to change this from employees who would prefer to work Sunday night rather than Friday night, and from others. I have found little support for observing the Sabbath from religious leaders. It has not been difficult to observe the Sabbath in the past. When there are clear inviolable constraints in the business, we find an alternative way to solve our problems. We do, for instance, work very hard and effectively during the week. However, it is fair to say that, with the lack of support from other Christians, working on the Sabbath may be allowed at some time in future.

The company has a strong work ethic which aligns with Christian principles. It is not just a puritan work ethic. The Catholic Church 'is convinced that work is a fundamental dimension of man's existence on earth', 'through work man must earn his daily bread' and that 'work is a good thing for man'.[5] In the company, work is understood as wealth creation which means, though we cannot be the judge of this, added value for our customers. The focus on the result brings people together and creates the team that enjoys the achievement which results. There can be real satisfaction in producing a new product, a faster delivery, a million parts without a reject, or gaining a new customer.

I have heard it said that employers often ask Christians to compromise on truth, integrity, and respecting God in each human being. As an employer, I try to support a culture where these values are central, both by setting an example myself and through supporting others. I try also to be open to correction by others when I have fallen short. Internally, this is much easier as the company makes the rules. When dealing with another party that does not play by the same rules, the temptation is to play the same game as the other party, particularly if it is a customer. A customer or supplier may not accept a charge that you think is completely justified, but, on the other hand, would pay for things that you do not consider to be justified or chargeable. Sometimes these are tradable, but the essential part is truth and honest accounting.

We should also be clear on the value that truth, integrity, keeping our promises and respecting others, have for the business. These values provide a foundation for the trust which allows a business to function far more efficiently, as there are many costs associated with a lack of trust (as has been noted by *The Economist* many years ago). The costs and time delays involved in the purchase of the factory (mentioned above) are but one example of additional costs incurred by lack of trust. In general, when we work with our suppliers and customers, we assume a high level of trust that people will do what they say they will do—something that is not always appreciated outside the business world. Trust is not a soft option. It is not something given but earned. It demands that commitments are delivered. The person who asks, 'Don't you trust me?' is often not to be trusted. I once visited a potential supplier to discuss a job. He told me what he could do, and I sent him an order which confirmed all the points he had committed to. His response was to phone me up, saying he did not want to be tied down in a contract; there had to be trust in business. This is not our idea of trust. Trust for us means standing by what you say. In fact he went out of business soon afterwards, breaking the trust that his creditors and others had placed in him.

Other than providing products and services that are needed, the company's responsibility to wider society is met, in the most part, by the taxes that are charged on its business and employment as rates, corporation tax, VAT, national insurance, and PAYE. The company also tithes its profits, giving the money to various charities. These contributions to society amount to something over £1M, or over £30K per person employed in the company, a figure which is in excess of take-home pay and dividends. In this respect, we can see that the company is more of a benefit to society in purely monetary terms than it is to its employees and shareholders.

SUMMARY

- In practice, little value is placed on the ownership of business in public companies. The owners devolve their duties to directors; their concern is shareholder value. In private companies, ownership has a real the possibility of wider responsibilities.

- A business is not just a device to create money for shareholders, it is an opportunity to contribute to the good of society. One way of doing this is through paying tax.
- The first responsibility of a business owner is to run a successful and profitable business.

- Equally important is honouring contracts, written or unwritten.
- Additionally, staying in business is essential: bankruptcy results in taking money from creditors.
- Fair pay is paying the market rate, keeping differentials reasonable, and allowing all employees to share in the profitability of the company. Rewards can be so arranged that there is no division between labour and capital.
- Sabbath observance puts work in its proper place. It has not been a problem for our company to observe the Sabbath.
- An employer can support a culture of truth, integrity, and respecting God in each human being.
- Trust makes for efficient working; it is not a soft option.
- Tax and the products made are the company's contribution to society.

NOTES

1. Rodney Green, *90,000 Hours* (Scripture Union: 2002), p. 13.
2. Joseph Fry was disowned by Ratcliff & Barking Monthly Meeting in May 1829; he was re-instated 1838 (source: Wikipedia, http://en.wikipedia.org/wiki/Joseph_Fry_(tea_merchant).
3. In the parable of the Workers in the Vineyard (Matthew 20.1–15) the owner of the vineyard hires casual workers at various times during the day; some work the whole day, others much shorter periods. When the first workers are hired at the beginning of the day the owner agrees to pay them 'the regular wage', *i.e.* enough for a man to live on for a day; as the other workers are hired he agrees to pay them 'a fair wage.' At the end of the day, all receive the same: the regular wage for a day's work. Those who have worked longest protest that the owner has made the others equal to them. The owner responds that they should not be jealous because he has decided to be generous; he has not cheated them, he has paid them the amount agreed. One way of

understanding this parable is that paying workers enough to live on is more important than preserving differentials. *(Ed.)*

4. *Laborem Exercens,* an Encyclical Letter of Pope John Paul II, published in 1981 to mark the ninetieth anniversary of *Rerum Novarum.* The quotations are from section 13.

5. *Laborem Exercens,* section 13.

10. THE HOUSING CONUNDRUM: TOWARDS A CONTINUUM

— Keith Croxton —

*I know that your goodness and love will
be with me all my life; and your house
will be my home as long as I live.*
PSALM 23.6 (GNB)

*People will build houses and get to live in
them—they will not be used by someone else.*
ISAIAH 65.21(GNB)

*You trample on the poor and force him to give
you grain. Therefore though you have built stone
mansions you will not live in them; though you have
planted lush vineyards you will not drink their wine.*
AMOS 5.11 (NIV)

The Psalmist and the Prophet saw the importance of a place of security, a place of belonging. Amos, railing at the injustice he saw in his community, pointed the finger at those who felt they were secure in their mansions whilst ignoring the plight of the poor. Their sense of security was illusionary; ultimately such selfishness was of no lasting value. Alan Wilson and Rosie Harper have also written about the illusion of wealth as a guarantor of security in an earlier chapter. Yet, it is interesting that Amos highlighted the mansions to point out the injustice and poverty that existed, and that these issues were linked some 2,700 years ago

Housing today is seen as a key part of the economic landscape, but, as Mullins and Murie point out, there are still ramifications in terms of society, justice, and politics.

> Housing can make both a direct and indirect contributions to poverty and social exclusion. Direct contributions include insufficient provision of shelter (homelessness and rooflessness), inadequate housing (poor physical conditions and overcrowding), and unresponsive housing policy and practices. Indirect contributions arise when housing circumstances increase the risk of social exclusion for example because of the location of housing or the relationship with local environments and services.[1]

The economic and social challenges facing someone who has no place to live—or who is at the bottom of the social scale—are formidable, and the way housing impacts on the wider economy not only exacerbates these challenges, but is a key factor in finding solutions. These challenges too often overwhelm as the housing maze is navigated by those striving—or being helped to strive—not only to achieve a more permanent place to live, but also seeking to become more self-sufficient economically: to be able to avail themselves of economic opportunities that become more easily accessible with a more permanent and stable lifestyle. Permanence and stability are not only important economically; St Benedict, as discussed by Alan Hargrave, stressed the absolute importance of stability for spiritual development.

Peter Sills has written about six values that provide the foundation for the theonomic approach being discussed. For example, he argues that equality in the Bible is the basic equality of every person in the sight of God, and, beyond that, how people are treated is a matter of justice. He also stresses the importance of 'the person in community', and the 'well being' of community. These, and the other values described, are relevant when exploring the never-ending issue of housing those in greatest need.

A number of factors have conspired to produce a class within society who are classified as homeless. The word 'homeless' is used to describe someone without a house, a roof over his or her head. The words 'house' and 'home' tend to be used interchangeably to refer to the physical building, but a different definition is needed to draw out the issues involved.

In this chapter, 'house' will be used to describe the physical building. For those seeking a house, this could be a self contained dwelling or accommodation provided by an organization such as Housing Associations, and may therefore be a room in a shared house.

'Home' will be used to describe what is created or takes place within the house. Home is where a person experiences development, both personal growth and life-skill development, and where you learn the values and ideals that can shape your life. Home can be a place of belonging, a place of security, a place of affirmation and compassion, a place of growth, a place where family and relationship is experienced, and a place that has emotional and spiritual meaning. A place to which one is drawn back, missed when away, and where roots can be planted. But sadly 'home' can also be a place of abuse, a place of isolation, a place of rejection. A cold place where self worth and value gets drummed out of a person. A place where emotional and spiritual needs are damaged or buried, a place to run away from or be thrown out of, a place of bad dreams and cruel memories. It is sad that so many who are seeking a house do so because home no longer exists. Broken relationships and rejection, for whatever reason, be it drugs, pregnancy, or a total implosion of communications, often lead to that person being on the street, looking for something that starts as a basic need: shelter.

There are, therefore, those who are in need of a house: they have no permanent place to live, they have been deprived of that physical building—they are houseless. Then there are those who have never experienced, or have been deprived of a home: they do not have a place where they feel they belong, or are drawn back to or where they would flee to in time of trouble—they are homeless. To assume that those without a house are just in need of a physical building is a damaging assumption because, if their experience of 'home' is generally destructive in terms of their personal growth and development, there will be social, emotional and spiritual needs as well. It is also interesting that the importance of the home as the foundational economic institution was central to Aristotle's concept of *Oikos*.

Even if it is accepted that people need a house and to experience a home, there is a wider need yet: a home can't be truly a home in isolation. There is within the human DNA a bias to live within, to feel part of, a community. At the heart of the Christian faith, developed and affirmed from Genesis to Revelation, is inter-relatedness and community. This, theologically, is what the Trinity expresses. To live in isolation or to feel no one cares is a painful and damaging experience; it is not a God-intended state. So, when tackling the needs of those without somewhere to live, we have to look beyond just the physical house to home-building and then to community. I believe we need to work to that continuum, house to home to community, recognising that many will need to be accompanied on that journey if it has any chance of being successful. This is a complex journey for those seeking to deliver such a service as well as for those making it. But to achieve the goal of someone no longer feeling excluded or at the margins, no longer totally dependent on others, including the state, for their financial and social support, but rather feeling part of a community they want to contribute to socially and economically has enormous benefits for them and the overall public good. The economist Hernando De Soto has written extensively about the power of property rights, and, in fact, claims that the development of the United States is largely due to the Homestead Act, under which squatters were given properties and all the rights that accrue from ownership.

Where we are now has developed over recent decades, through numerous government headlines, policies and initiatives. I want to examine some of the pressures and issues the different parts of the continuum throw up, which makes the journey through it so complex, to look at some examples of what can be achieved, and to ask whether they provide pointers to help move society towards something more economically, socially, and spiritually holistic.

10.1. HOUSE

The provision of a house for all its citizens is a fundamental mark of a society that believes in justice and compassion; it affirms the value and uniqueness of each person. A just, compassionate society has to care for all its members, and the provision of a permanent place to live is a key part of a holistic approach to creating such a society.

The lack of a permanent place to live, or having no place to live, for so many people remains a scar on our society. Temporary accommodation is not a solution, economically or emotionally. The lack of permanence, often involving the threat of being thrown out at short notice, does not provide the opportunity or motivation to start the journey along the continuum. Permanence also begins to open the door to employment and education during that crucial home building stage.

Two factors that have a significant impact on the price of a house are supply and affordability. The demand for housing is increasing. The continuing rise in the population, the breakdown of relationships, people living longer and single parent families are some of the changes in society that are contributing to this increasing demand. The current shortfall in the supply of housing, and, in particular, the decline in building provision by social landlords, has put pressure on the private rental sector. This has been added to by the increase in those renting for the first time because of the tighter mortgage controls during the current economic crisis. These factors will drive the price of housing the 'houseless' higher.

Today, many people see a house as an investment. Property has traditionally been seen as a good investment for the homeowner or the professional investor. For some, it is a way of making a profit, for others a pension provision, or a way of climbing up the property ladder and being seen as upwardly mobile. Second homes have also become part of this scene, again used for short-term profit through renting or as a long-term investment—buy at the right time, sell at the right time. For this culture of property investment to work, the pressure is for house prices to rise. This upward pressure to see a profit from a house is part of the wider drive for financial 'success' across the economy, and this raises the question of whether an unfettered accumulation of 'riches' does more harm than good.

The price of a house is also seen as an important measure of the economic state of the country. If the price is rising then the economy is seen to be healthy, the 'feel factor' is said to be good— except that there are costs, but these are rarely mentioned in this context. Rises in the cost of housing cause increased debt through mortgages and add to the pressure for wage and benefits increases, the latter, in turn, adding to the cost of the benefits system. If, however, the rise to benefits is contained, or curtailed, by capping, then more are driven into poverty or forced to move to a cheaper area. But what is the problem: the price of the house or the benefit rate? Either way, for those at the bottom of the housing ladder, it just gets harder.

The cost/availability of mortgages is a further measure used to check the economic pulse. Ever-increasing house prices funded by readily available mortgages was seen as a sign of a healthy economy. This presented opportunities for financial institutions to make unreasonable gains via mortgages through their willingness to offer ever-increasing mortgages to those who did not have the resources to handle that debt, which has had disastrous consequences. Debt was good until that particular house of cards fell with a rather large crash. Unfettered debt accumulation damages not only the economy but also the individual. As Daniel Doring rightly points out, 'usury laws are ancient religious laws banning profiteering from interest payments on debts. All human societies have found money lending for profit leads to great injustice.'[2] The debt-fuelled upward rise in house prices added to the debt, inequality, and injustice for those at the bottom even though they were not the key participants in this economic tragedy.

The price of land and the opportunities for greed amongst the many players in the housing system have also impacted on the affordability of a house. Unfettered greed by individuals or businesses shows morality is of little consequence, and eventually hits those who are at the bottom of the economic ladder. As Daniel Doring points out, greed ultimately corrupts:

> We have to say again and again that there are no beneficial side effects of one man's greed. It does not create worthwhile work for others; it is not efficient; it does not control waste; in fact it causes huge amounts to be wasted. Greed also corrupts thinking as those who take most simultaneously argue that they fund state services the most through taxes they cannot avoid.[3]

The current supply and affordability issues discussed create serious problems for those struggling to find a permanent place to live. As Mullins and Murie highlight, there was also a long standing problem simmering within society even before the latest economic crisis: 'With the growth of home ownership and the contribution of social renting there has been a growing concentration of economically inactive, less skilled, unemployed and low income people in social housing.'[4]

The fact this concentration exists within our society is because successive social and economic systems have failed to solve the root causes. The financial and political cost to roll back decades of insular housing, educational and social policies that have created these deprived, benefit dependant, communities will prohibit the root and branch surgery needed. And yet, for the long-term health of the economy, major surgery is needed.

10.2. HOME

The provision of a house is a physical response, and is a crucial first stage for those who are 'houseless', but there are emotional, social and economic needs that have be to be addressed as well. The next step in the continuum is that of home building, the time where people can begin to get a vision of a future for themselves, for the first time, perhaps, to begin to dream of what might be possible, and have aspirations for a new kind of life. So often they have come from a world where they saw nothing beyond survival, where claiming benefits was a way of life, and where a chaotic lifestyle was too often the norm. To open their eyes to new possibilities, and to deliver what is needed to bring them about, means intense support during this development phase. As Timothy Keller points out, this development stage can be life changing and crucial in moving those at the margins into community:

> Development is more about what is needed to bring a person or community to self sufficiency. In the Old Testament when a slave's debt was erased and he was released, God directed that his former master send him out with grain, tools and resources for a new, self sufficient economic life.
>
> *Deuteronomy 15.12–15*

> Development includes for example providing education, job creation and training, housing development and home ownership and so on in community.[5]

To help someone move towards being a person in community, economically and emotionally, will involve training, mentoring, counselling and resources. But this cannot be tackled in a bureaucratic, tick box, attitude. It demands a non-judgemental attitude and a willingness to serve with unconditional love and compassion by those who believe every person has the right to reach their God-given potential. It demands the radical form of *agape* that Andrew Lightbown and Nick Fane have written about in Chapter 7. It also requires a clear and positive strategy to move people through the continuum. It will involve, in particular, having organizations that are willing to invest in the homebuilding/ development stage of the continuum.

There is another factor that has to be recognised. There is a health cost as the lack of a permanent home, and the feelings of helplessness and injustice, overwhelm those in that situation.

> Human beings are not mentally immune to the effects of rising elitism, exclusion, prejudice and greed. It is because we can now measure how humans have reacted, and where they have reacted most badly, that many now claim with great conviction that all the injustices and inequalities which underlie most rich societies are having a 'dose response' effect in the mental well-being of the population: the greater the dose of inequality the higher the response in terms of poor mental health.[6]

If we are to move people from a sense of isolation and helplessness, from feeling rejected and angry at being marginalized, from being benefits-dependent, from poor health to well-being, we have to help them create a home: a place they want to come back to each day, where they can begin to experience a sense of belonging and security a safe place where they can be helped to develop their life skills, and have their social, emotional, medical and spiritual needs addressed in more lasting ways.

10.3.   COMMUNITY

Homes are the building blocks of community. It is the interrelatedness of homes that create a community. Community is more than building houses; it is about creating an environment where there are shared values, mutual acceptance, support and care. If we are to move someone towards emotional and economic self-sufficiency, then being part of community, being a 'person in community', is crucial.

The lack of joined-up thinking between housing, social, and educational policies has created housing concentrations based on affordability. Thus we have monochrome communities at all levels of society. This has been damaging to those communities and individuals at the bottom of the social scale, and, economically, there are significant costs to maintaining those communities through social, economic and medical support. It is interesting that those Victorian industrialists who built model villages had a holistic vision of what was needed to build communities, as Ian Bradley has said: 'For the employees of Salts, Cadbury, Rowntrees and Lever Brothers the firm was a provider of not just wages but of housing, healthcare, education, recreation and entertainment.'[7]

They also believed that the way they built communities could tackle the social problems of their day. It might seem quirky in our time, but, to tackle the alcohol problem, they refused to have public houses in their villages—their aim was to deal with a perceived destructive influence on the communities they were building. By contrast, today communities are shaped and stereotyped by the problems within, and this fires feelings of injustice and seclusion. Finding a way of rediscovering holistic communities will need new thinking and resources, as Malpass and Rowland point out: 'If we are to regain our supposed lost communities, rebuild neighbourhoods that work, or develop a better functioning urban fabric, it is vital that the various yet complex strands needed to realise the vision are brought together. Disparate and disjointed policies, together with the need to satisfy dominant beneficiaries, amount to less sustainable communities.'[8]

These are just some of the issues that reverberate around the housing conundrum, and have to be faced by those at the bottom of the housing ladder as well as those helping them. Each part of the continuum—house, home, community—has a set of problems that need to be accepted and addressed if we are to see any change to the housing landscape.

Faced with this, how can the Christian community respond? What can it bring to the table? Can a different economic approach, as Peter Sills suggests, begin to deal with the injustices and inequalities in housing? Rodney Stark believes that the Christian community was initially a revitalising movement that opened up new ways and ideas for transforming the lives and situations of those in greatest need:

> Christianity served as a revitalization movement that arose in response to the misery, chaos, fear and brutality of life in the urban Greco-Roman world. Christianity revitalised life in . . . cities by providing new norms and new kinds of social relationships able to cope with many urgent urban problems. To cities filled with the homeless and impoverished Christianity offered charity as well as hope. To cities filled with newcomers and strangers, Christianity offered an immediate basis for attachment . . . Christianity offered a new basis for social solidarity.[9]

The transforming features of that movement are just as important in our time. New norms and new kinds of social relationships are needed if the deep-rooted problems in the housing world, with the related social and poverty issues, are to be resolved. A fresh understanding of what charity means within the economy, so that hope can be restored to those in greatest need, is also key.

The norms and social relationships that exist within the deprived communities are alien to other communities, and are thus kept at arm's length, but it needs to be recognised that these norms have been created by policies and benefit systems designed by those living to a very different set of norms. To remove injustice is not moving someone from one set of norms to our 'better set', rather it is about creating a new approach to community which has a transformed view of what community means: new norms, new social relationships, new understanding of solidarity, and a generosity that provides freedom to giver and receiver.

To become such a transforming movement again there are two strategies that could be offered:

10.3.1. To be a plumb line

Amos had a vision of God standing by a wall built true to plumb holding a plumb line in his hand; he said that hwas going to set a plumb line among his people (Amos 7.7–9). Only when it is set against that which is true can society see how far it falls short of God's values and ideals, and what flaws need to be addressed. Amos saw that prosperity was not just about economics, but that there were spiritual, physical, exclusion and moral elements as well.

J. A. Motyer, in his commentary on Amos, cites the 'social offences' that Amos sees in Israel's society.[10] He attacks:

- acquisitiveness which allows the end to justify the means
- ruling classes becoming self-important and callous
- wealth as only a means of luxury for some to the neglect of those less well supplied
- perversion of justice in the courts
- commercial dishonesty
- the inhumanity of big business when it treats people as commodities

For Amos, these offences were a window into the soul of his nation. His attack was aimed at a moral and spiritual disease that had corrupted the God-given imperatives for human community. Unless these were addressed injustice would continue to prevail. Rabbi Jonathan Sacks underlines this in our time by adding that ignoring these elements will create individuals and communities where serious problems will fester: . . . the economics and politics of globalization have an inescapable moral dimension. Their aim must be to enhance, not compromise human dignity . . . economic systems create problems that cannot be resolved by economics alone . . . there is no escape from the wider issues of morality and if we ignore them history suggests that they will return in the form of anger, resentment and a burning sense of injustice.[11]

This burning sense of injustice is not helped by the phrase 'the undeserving poor'. This moral judgement is hollow and hypocritical unless accompanied by a similar injunction: the 'undeserving rich'. It is immoral to bear down on one and not the other. Passages such as this one from Deuteronomy point to an economic culture where generosity comes before judging, and the well-being of individual members is the concern of the whole:

> When in any of your settlements in the land which the Lord your God is giving you one of your fellow-countrymen becomes poor, do not be hard-hearted or close-fisted towards him in his need. Be open-handed towards him and lend him on pledge as much as he needs . . . Give generously to him and do not begrudge him your bounty, because it is for this very bounty that the Lord your God will bless you in everything you do or undertake. The poor will always be with you in your land and that is why I command you to be open-handed towards any of your countrymen there who are in poverty and need.
>
> *Deuteronomy 15.7–11*

It would be easy to say such sentiments are of no relevance to our time and thus ignore them. But it is for the Church to interpret such values and directives so they can speak into our society. Until there is a new national soul which is marked by an accepted imperative that the wealthy have a moral responsibility for the well-being of the poor, and that the transformation of the lives of all its people is paramount, there will be little chance of removing the injustices and inequalities that plague those seeking a place to live.

Drawing on an Old Testament directive, Tom Sedlacek offers an interesting observation:

> In the Old Testament it was commanded that once every seven years the soil had to be left to rest. Aside from letting the ground lie fallow having certain agrarian benefits, the meaning of the commandment is much deeper. Once every seven years debt slaves (Hebrews who were indebted so much they fell into slavery) were freed from their slave

labour. Once every forty-nine years debts were forgiven and the land returned to its original tribal families. Simply once in a while the accumulation of wealth was erased. There was so to speak a systematic reset, restart or more modernly, reboot.[12]

There comes a time in the life of any society when to 'reboot' should be seen as a sensible, God-given directive. The Church needs to find its prophetic voice to set the plumb line before our society. Housing, along with its social, political and economic ramifications, is an important window into the soul of the nation, and the moral and spiritual disease of our time has to be discerned and confronted.

10.3.2. To model new ways to make a difference

As well as being a prophetic voice, it is crucial the Christian community grapples with the issues that exist in the housing arena. To explore how this can be done I want to look at what one Christian-based organization is trying to achieve.

Chapter 1 Housing Association is trying to make a difference through tackling the three parts of the continuum in a variety of contexts. Their motivation is rooted in their declared intention never to walk away from the vulnerable and homeless, whatever the economic pressures and constraints, and, through faith and creativity, find solutions to help those journeying to fulfil their God-given potential and find a home within community. Underpinning the work is a set of principles which shape the way *Chapter 1* operates; these are set out in the form of a credo as follows:

> **Credo**
> We believe . . .
> that lives don't have to stay the same and that everyone,
> given the time, space and opportunities, can become
> the person they themselves aspire to be and whom God

created them to be.
We believe . . .
that we can all be part of bringing lasting change to lives
that might seem hopelessly broken, bruised or lonely.
We believe . . .
that by working together, side by side, we can help
change the lives of people one by one.
We believe . . .
that although change happens, we don't always see it
instantly; it can be a slow and painful process and can
take time to be seen, but we always retain our hope in
the individual.

Mother Teresa was once asked if she really believed she could solve world hunger. She replied that she could, and, when asked how she could possibly do that, her reply was simple: one person at a time. *Chapter 1*'s strap line is 'changing lives one by one', and it this approach that can lift any sense of hopelessness that individuals experience when faced with all the issues involved in moving towards functional interdependence. This bottom-up relational approach followed by *Chapter 1*, and typified by Mother Theresa, when backed up by a supportive and creative top-down policies (currently lacking), could make a real difference.

Meanwhile, this focused approach can provide the framework to achieve real progress thorough the continuum. Martin Batstone, Chaplain of *Chapter 1*, underlines the commitment needed when he talks about the theology underpinning the work of *Chapter 1*. He stresses there has to be a deep sense of calling by those supporting and helping because there are times when it is necessary to go beyond the provision of state or societal convention, and be challenged by the outsider and the vulnerable. Systems and structures that are designed to care too often fail. They become brittle, lose focus, become too politicised and weighed down with bureaucracy, and even become corrupt. Ann Morisy gives theological language to the response. There has to be a pattern of discipleship that is ready to take up the cross, in terms of making a positive choice to engage in the struggle for justice. Only when we can stand alongside and identify with outsider is the cross made real.

> Taking up the cross means we have continually to ask questions which make those who are powerful uncomfortable . . . Taking up the cross and following Jesus means unmasking dishonest assumptions and practices as well as expressing care for those in need, whether they be those whom society subtly casts as deserving or undeserving.[13]

Chapter 1 Housing Association is committed to standing alongside those seeking to move through the continuum. Achieving successful outcomes means addressing each part of that continuum in new ways as the economic and social landscape changes. Working amongst the homeless and vulnerable is a tough financial environment; it is not a business where quick profits can be made. It requires business stamina and an 'extra mile' ethos.[14] There have to be robust business cases and models with tightly controlled cost management, but that is about good stewardship of God-given resources. Two recent developments provide examples of what can be achieved, and both of these projects 'wash their faces' financially. These examples are included to highlight the importance of affordability, stability and development on the journey into community.

In Cornwall, *Chapter 1* has reached an agreement with a number of private social landlords, which ensures an affordable rent charged to those needing a house, in exchange for *Chapter 1* guaranteeing the rent, and monitoring and managing the tenants. The aim is to provide affordable permanent accommodation where *Chapter 1* staff can give the intense support, training and mentoring required to help residents develop the confidence and skills needed to move towards independence within community.

In Buckingham, a local church was deeply concerned about the plight of the homeless in their community. They approached *Chapter 1*, which was able to purchase six properties in partnership with local and central government agencies. Volunteers from the local churches helped get the houses ready for the first residents to move in, and are now involved in the second stage of the continuum, the home-building. The volunteers have been able to build relationships and help the residents develop the life skills they need to move towards coping, as well as helping them become part of the wider community.

In both of these examples each part of the continuum was addressed. Affordability was the first challenge, then the intense mentoring and support that enabled development to take place, and finally, the move towards community both within the project and then into the wider community. Both these models can easily be rolled out to other towns and areas; indeed, this is already happening. A key factor could be local churches/communities wanting to respond to the homeless and vulnerable in their area, taking that responsibility on themselves, and not relying on the statutory bodies to solve the problems. Working in partnership with organizations involved in the work elsewhere can bring about real change in individuals and communities. Two stories from the initiatives mentioned illustrate what can be achieved in the lives of individuals.

A & B and their three children lost their council home of 25 years after A became seriously ill, confined to a wheelchair, and was no longer able to work. Her husband had to give up work to care for her. During this very difficult time, they failed to get to grips with the complex benefit system and, subsequently, fell into serious arrears with their rent, leading to their eviction. A's mental health also suffered greatly during this time; the family were in despair, split up, sofa surfing with different friends and family, and living from carrier bags. Fortunately *Chapter 1* we were able to offer the family a home through the Private Sector Leasing scheme. Staff, aware of the prior circumstances, supported the family intensely with benefit claims and budgeting plans to reduce other large debts that had accumulated. Finally, having established a stable home environment, A was able to seek the medical help she needed and begin recovery. Two years on, A has made such progress that her husband is now back at work. They can now begin to build their lives from a position of stability and hope.

C was living in a tent with her partner in the garden of relatives. They also had a child. The local Health Visitor was alarmed by their situation and approached *Chapter 1*. They were housed in one the six *Chapter 1* houses available, and supported by volunteers who helped them with the life skills they needed to manage a home. That home is now well established, and C is now actively involved in the local community, helping at two local charities.

These are two success stories—and there are many others that could be told—that show how lives can be changed. Sadly there are failures as well, much to the distress of those working with those involved.

There are no easy answers as to how this deep-seated issue can be addressed and resolved, so, inevitably, we are scratching the surface. Just as we need economic entrepreneurs, there is a crying need for a resurgence of community entrepreneurs who can bring new ways of economic and social thinking to the table. It's worth remembering that Christian reformers and entrepreneurs have, down the centuries, broken the norms and accepted values of societies to bring about new ways of relieving injustice, poverty and corruption. Their motivation was rooted in their strong beliefs that there are certain God-given values and directives about how humans should live together and treat each other.

There is a need for a version of 'model villages' that can show how communities can still be built that will solve problems rather than create them, that are able to move people into a holistic community culture in which being a person in community and economic well-being can both be achieved. Such communities could be based on an agreed covenant setting out an accepted set of moral and ethical principles underpinning the development. Covenant is a significant feature of the Old Testament. It speaks of relationship and mutual trust within a religious and moral framework; it also reinforces interrelatedness. Such an approach might open new ways of creating community where difference is embraced rather than seen as an opportunity for division.

The 'model' for our time could see investors and entrepreneurs investing in people and communities rather than simply in profit-making opportunities. National and local investment vehicles could be created which would enable individuals, local community groups and businesses to respond to the needs of the houseless/homeless. This direct involvement of responding to a social need, rather than via taxes, might open up new ways of solving this long-standing social problem. Both of the models described lend themselves to investor involvement, and such an investment movement might challenge wider economic thinking. It would be interesting if a small number of such investment investment-style communities could be piloted to test whether this approach would open up new ways of tackling the housing issues discussed.

The housing conundrum is one that will continue to impact on the moral and economic well-being of our society until there is a transformation within the soul of the nation that will open up a more honest acceptance of the issues involved. Amos called his people back to God-given values about community and selflessness which had to be in place before renewal and restoration could be experienced. There are solutions, but they need to come from a different heart.

SUMMARY

- Housing is a key factor within the economy, but tackling the lack of adequate housing means addressing difficult and engrained social, justice and political issues.
- To understand the plight of those without some kind of permanent accommodation, or wanting to move towards a more self sufficient life, it is important to recognise the three stages of a continuum that need to be addressed: house, home and community. The provision of a house is not sufficient on its own.

- Unfettered debt, greed, and accumulation of wealth are root causes of the injustices that impact on housing, and that make the journey through the continuum complex and overwhelming without help.
- It is questionable whether communities based on the affordability of properties contribute to social cohesion and overall economic well-being. But to move towards more mixed/diverse communities is more than just house building, it requires a transformed view of community building.
- Local community organizations/businesses/churches can be instrumental in identifying those without a permanent house/home and inviting those already with experience in solving such problems to work in partnership to make a real difference
- There is a need for community investors/entrepreneurs to bring new economic thinking to community development. New national and local investment vehicles would be needed to support such an approach.
- Until there is a new national soul which is marked by an accepted imperative that the wealthy have a moral responsibility for the well being of the poor, and that the transformation of the lives of all its people is paramount, there will be little chance of removing the injustices and inequalities that plague those seeking a place to live.

NOTES

1. David Mullins & Alan Murie, *Housing Policy in the UK* (Palgrave Macmillan: 2006), p. 254. Reproduced with permission of Palgrave Macmillan.
2. Daniel Doring, *Injustice—why social inequality persists* (Policy Press: Bristol, 2011), p. 218.
3. Ibid, p. 29.

4. David Mullins & Alan Murie, *Housing Policy in the UK*, p. 258. Reproduced with permission of Palgrave Macmillan.
5. Timothy Keller, *Gospel in Life* (Zondervan: 2010), p. 114. Copyright © Redeemer City to City and Redeemer Presbyterian Church, 2010.
6. Daniel Doring, *Injustice—why social inequality persists*, p. 269.
7. 'For the employees of Salts' extract taken from Ian Bradley, *Enlightened Entrepreneurs in Victorian Britain* (Lion Press: 2007), p. 11. Copyright © Ian Bradley, 2007. Reproduced with permission of Lion Hudson Plc.
8. Pete Malpass & Bob Rowlands (eds.), *Housing Markets and Policy* (Routledge: 2010), p. 219.
9. Rodney Stark, *The Rise of Christianity* (Harper: New York, 1997), p. 161.
10. J. A. Motner's article on *Amos* is in the *New Bible Commentary* (IVP Press: 2005), p. 792.
11. Jonathan Sacks, *The Dignity of Difference* (Continuum: 2002), pp. 3–4. Copyright © Jonathan Sacks. Reproduced with permission of Continuum, an imprint of Bloomsbury Publishing Plc.
12. Tomas Sedlacek, *Economics of Good and Evil* (Oxford University Press: Oxford, 2011), p. 245. Reproduced by permission of Oxford University Press, USA.
13. Ann Morisy, *Beyond the Good Samaritan: Community ministry and mission* (Mowbray: 1997), p. 109. Copyright © Ann Morisy. Reproduced with permission of Mowbray, an imprint of Bloomsbury Publishing Plc.
14. The 'extra mile' ethos is inspired by Jesus' words in the Sermon on the Mount: 'If someone in authority presses you into service for one mile, go with him two.' (Matthew 5.41) This is one of several sayings of Jesus about the importance of generous, rather than calculated, responses.

11. SCHOOL FOR THE LORD'S SERVICE

— **Richard Backhouse** —

The mind is not a vessel to be filled,
but a fire to be kindled.
PLUTARCH

There has, perhaps, been no period in history when the juxtaposition of faith and education has been so contentious. The modern-day faith school finds itself sandwiched between the past—where the value, existence and institutionalization of education relied more on faith than anything else—and the future—where one can reasonably expect the nature of any faith in the lives of young people to be increasingly regulated by the state. In the play *Jumpers*, first performed in 1972, one character observes that, at some stage, there was '. . . a calendar date—a moment when the onus of proof passed from the atheist to the believer, when, quite suddenly the noes had it.'[1] It is not only a ghetto mentality within the (British, at any rate) Christian Church that has led to a pessimism about the extent to which the state will allow matters of faith to be discussed in an educational context, let alone permit a faith-based context to be the appropriate venue (emotionally, as well as geographically) for education to take place. The exclusion of Religious Studies from the English Baccalaureate in 2010/11 is just one sign of the extent to which secularists have sought to expunge faith from the public square.[2]

As a result of this hostility many schools have reduced the level at which faith plays out in their communities to the historical root of their value systems. Leaders of these schools quote CS Lewis: 'Education without values . . . seems rather to make man a more clever devil.'[3] This chapter seeks rather to ask what a school would look like if the institution were to seek to embed the Christian faith in its workings at the deepest level. No fixed conclusion is offered by this author—instead the reader may find it helpful, as the author did, to think of one of those graphs, used to torture pupils aged 15, in which inequalities ($x > 5$, for example) are expressed by the ruling out (with cross hatching) of some areas of possibility, while other areas are explicitly left open. When several different areas are ruled out, there exists a space in which all potential solutions may be found. In this case, the 'space' left is still large enough for schools to be creative, to be different from one other, and still to be distinctively Christian. A School for the Lord's Service is not a blueprint—it does not provide for a single static solution.

Furthermore, paradoxically, this chapter does not consider how lessons should be delivered in the classroom, principally because others have written at greater length on such matters, most notably David Smith.[4]

The author ought further to preface his remarks by pointing the reader to his biography—his observations need to be read in the context of his role leading a fee-paying school which seeks to provide an education which is on protestant and evangelical principles in accordance with the doctrines of the Church of England. Indeed, this is a school which was founded for the children of missionaries and clergy, and which sought to educate children to be missionaries; and still does.

Within this context, the following values are seen in our context as axiomatic, although many are counter-cultural:

1. Of central importance is the belief that the value of each child is of greater importance than the 'output' of each child; in other words, their character matters more than their achievements or deeds. Christian faith provides the clearest value of each human being, situated within the love which God has shown humans in the life, and death, of Jesus. Such value, expressed for all people, is also understandable in the context of, and applicable to, each person as an individual. As Christians, therefore, our value of ourselves is founded

on God's value—on our creation and redemption—rather than on our activity. The alternative, possibly demonstrated most clearly in achievement-dominated selective day schools, may lead to a life which continues to need to be fed by ongoing achievement in order to function. Many former pupils of such schools report a mid-life crisis as the result of a self-value based on achievement—for there is nothing to provide a sense of personal value at exactly that moment when it is needed, when there has been a pause in achievement. The work of Simon Walker, illustrated in his 'Undefended Leadership' trilogy, makes multiple references to the burn-out that can (and often does) follow from the pursuit of achievement as the highest goal.[5] He situates his model of leadership within the paradigm established by Goffman—the front stage and the back stage of our lives. The front stage may be summarized as 'doing', and is 'presented' (i.e. visible), and the back stage summarized as 'being', and is 'reserved' (i.e. largely hidden), and, if it is shown, it is only in private. A school for the Lord's service must be a community which embodies the belief that self-value is intrinsic, non-negotiable, and arising out of our nature and our variety as human beings, rather than out of achievement. A consequence of this truth is that pastoral care becomes a core part of education, because it communicates what the institution values. School is about learning to 'do life' well. Pastoral care is not—as is implied by the Every Child Matters agenda[6]—important only because it is one of the means to improve academic output. Caring for people and communicating value to them is one of the key functions of educational institutions. It is not merely a pun to suggest that what adults value will be absorbed by children as their values. It is essential that an organization which says human beings matter because they are human-beings outworks that principle in its care for young people—in patience, in an ongoing belief in the possibility of redemption, and in the provisions made for pupils pastorally.

2. The Christian theology of a school can—indeed, should— also provide a clear (and fairly non-negotiable) idea of what are the desirable qualities to draw out of young people, and how structures operating in the school can do this. An over- dependence on competitive sport can be ruled out, because it places the outcome above relationships in the hierarchy of values. Community activities assume more value because they teach altruism, collaboration, thoughtfulness and a servant-leader approach to problem-solving. Of course, many organizations can claim this, but what they lack, if the values are not underpinned by theology, is any means to prevent this anchor from slipping over time. The role of education is not simply to educate young people in a manner reflective of contemporary culture, but to lead thinking. Sometimes, leadership involves being the last to change rather than the first to do so. Weber's work suggests that, while institutions might try to protect this erosion by establishing policies and protocols to embed values, such initiatives actually lead to the bureaucracy replacing the values they are designed to protect since bureaucrats are rendered automatons by the bureaucratic machinery.[7] A theological anchor is vital.

3. Schools need to view children as 'missionaries', not factories. Schools have a unique place to envision young people as to the value that they can bring to bear on the world. Again, where contemporary culture may teach them that the purpose of their lives is to fill their pockets, a school for the Lord's service might be able to inspire young people to be a gift to world. It is important, however, to emphasise that some people are gifts to the world by means of their willingness to share their economic success—trade is not 'dirty'. Nevertheless, giving young people a vision that their gifts are so called not because they are exclusively for their own benefit but also for the benefit of their community, however that might be defined, is a value that must inform the whole of the school's working. This 'solidarity' (as

Andrew Lightbown calls it) is greater than the solidarity of care for each other; it is an economic solidarity which demands that we all use our gifts for the greatest good of mankind, not merely of ourselves (Adam Smith's invisible hand does have significant limitations!).

4. This view of pupils leads to another conclusion: schools should have an expectation that their public benefit as an institution will arise principally from the working life of former pupils (actually, this is the very reason education is classified as a 'merit good'). A school that can generate 'salt' and 'light' from its former pupils can expect to be a massive lever for public good, whether its pupils go on to be missionaries, clergy, social workers, hedge fund managers, lorry drivers, or HR managers.

5. A school for the Lord's service must be unselfish about its own role in the lives of young people; too often schools behave as if the experience of the pupil at school is all that matters. One Headteacher for whom once I worked, related the story of an elderly gentleman whom he had met at his school, and whose own son had attended the school some years previously. As the meeting of the Governors at which the school's fees were set was looming, the Head asked the elderly man if he considered the expenditure on the fees to have been money well spent. 'My dear chap,' replied the elderly gentleman, 'my son is only 40; it's much too soon to tell!' An expectation that an education should pay a dividend over a child's whole lifetime (and beyond!) is fitting. For readers whose reaction to an anecdote predicated on fee-paying education is adverse, I would note that the value of this anecdote is that it suggests that, since all education demands resources, evaluation of whether those resources have been well spent as the child leaves the school (or even as they reach the age of 40) is too short-termist. The school is merely the menu, and not the meal.

6. Finally, it is axiomatic that a Christian institution should demonstrate an essentially generous approach to its own

intellectual property rights. Of course, the 'worker deserves his pay,' (Luke 10.7) but copyright is too often used in a profit-culture as the right to a dividend in perpetuity. There is a big difference to the way that our culture treats the copyright on a textbook, or a course of study, and an engineering patent.

By contrast a school for the Lord's service might regard some territory as being ruled out:

1. Activities which merely fill pupils with dollops of knowledge, or are valuable only because they seek to make pupils more economically productive units, are not appropriate, even if other institutions are marketing themselves on the strength of these. In a similar way, mere teaching to the test should be anathema. The process of teaching is to facilitate the discovery of the wonders of creation, of the imagination of the human mind, or the work of the history, and never merely the accumulation of human capital. Thomas Gradgrind does not prosper in a Christian institution.[8] In fact, any kind of utilitarianism, let alone Benthamism, should be regarded with great suspicion.[9]

2. Such a school needs to consider carefully its basis for the selection of pupils. Very nearly all independent schools would take a highly academic route to selection if they could. Many maintained sector schools would do the same if they were able to, and some do so by other means. A highly academically selective approach to entry, or a monocular approach to pupil, or institutional, target-setting is not consistent with the value that should be placed on each person as described above. The issue of pupil selection is, therefore, a much more difficult aspect than it appears because the breadth of pupils' needs has a significant resource implication, particularly in smaller educational providers. No educational establishment should take students on courses they are bound to fail; resources which are expended

in doing so cannot then be made available to other students, whose opportunity to benefit would be greater. In addition, selection poses the problem that it reduces the value of the school as an introduction to the whole variety of God's creation, and it introduces a funny idea of reality to those students who are admitted—anyone who has heard students at Oxford or Cambridge describe themselves as 'thick' will understand the extent of this distortion of perception.

3. Finally, a school for the Lord's service is not merely a market-led organization which must respond to the whims of its customers. The education 'market', whether public or private, is one in which every pupil brings funding to the organization. This means that schools must fill themselves up to take advantage of the economies of scale available and to capture all the revenue which they can. This approach, on its own, can lead to an institution interpreting being business-like in its approach to mean that it must be parent-led to the point of vacuity. A school for the Lord's service, by contrast, is clearly concerned with higher authority, and while it should respect the authority parents have over their children, and their knowledge of their children, the school should also be forthright in asserting the principles on which it stands, and stand firm on those.

There are two further notes worth making in closing. First, of course, any institution within a theo-economy which recognizes the world through a Christian worldview should not be surprised to see Christian truth being outworked in the life of the organization. Of all the organizations, therefore, a genuinely theonomic one should never be complacent, recognizing, at least, the possibilities implied by the doctrine of original sin in all its dealings—at all levels. As much as—no, more than—anywhere else, the wisdom of Solomon (which was not, of course, his wisdom at all) is necessary to make judgments in the many areas of school life which normally give rise to tension and contention. All too often, such decisions revolve around the compromises that can be made between what is in the interest of the individual and what is in the interest of the community. Indeed, the post-modern priority of the needs and importance of the individual make these and other aspects of living in a community more tricky than ever, but that is the subject of another chapter.

Secondly, it would be unsurprising to find less alienation—that Christian term hijacked by Marx—among the teenagers at a school for the Lord's service than elsewhere (and this is our experience). Perhaps part of the reason teenagers are so afflicted by a cultural, social and spiritual alienation in our national life is that they cannot see the point, and neither can anyone explain it to them. In a Christian context, the point is always clear, or should be.

SUMMARY

- The juxtaposition of faith and education is more contentious today than it has been at any other time in history; secularists seek to expunge faith from the public sphere, and many schools have reduced the part that faith plays in their communities.
- In contrast, a 'School for the Lord's Service' seeks to embed the Christian faith in its workings; it does not offer a blueprint, but it does raise some vital—and counter-cultural—questions about the nature and form of education.
- Basic is the conviction that the value of each child is more important than the 'output' of each child; education loses sight of its purpose if it becomes 'achievement-dominated'.
- Being embedded in the Christian faith gives clarity to the desirable qualities to be drawn out of young people. Policies and protocols alone are not enough.
- Schools need to view children as 'missionaries', not factories, envisioning them to be a gift to the world.
- A school's value to the world is in the working lives of its

pupils.
- A school for the Lord's service is not primarily concerned to fill pupils with knowledge to make them more economically productive; selection is not based solely on academic criteria, and it is not a market-led organization responding to the needs of its customers.

NOTES

1. Tom Stoppard, *Jumpers* (George, Act 1), (Faber & Faber, 1972).
2. The exclusion of Religious Studies from the English Baccalaureate was announced in the Statement of Intent 2010—addendum (the english baccalaureate), published on-line by the DfE: www.education.gov.uk/performancetables/Statement-of-Intent-2010-Addendum.pdf
3. C.S. Lewis, *The Abolition of Man* (Harper Collins; New York, [1944] 1947). Copyright © CS Lewis Pte Ltd 1943, 1946, 1978.
4. David Smith & Barbara Carvill, *The Gift of the Stranger: Faith, Hospitality and Language Learning* (Eerdmans; Grand Rapids, 2000).
5. Simon P. Walker, *The Undefended Leader Trilogy* (Simon P Walker, 2011), Book 1, Ch. 3.
6. DfE, *Every Child Matters* (DfE: 2004, www.education.gov.uk/publications/standard/ publicationDetail/Page1/DfES/1081/2004
7. John Keane, in *Public Life and Late Capitalism* (CUP: Cambridge, 1984), explores the way in which bureaucracy can subvert the values it is meant to protect.
8. Thomas Gradgrind, a character in Charles Dickens' novel *Hard Times* (Household Words, 1854), is the headmaster of a school in which industrial revolution efficiency and industrial relations are transplanted.
9. 'Benthamism' is hard-line utilitarianism, named after the British philosopher and jurist Jeremy Bentham (1748–1832).

AFTERWORD: A PERSONAL REFLECTION

— Peter Sills —

We began with the ethical deficit in modern economic life which the banking crisis laid bare, but since then it has become clear that this deficit is not confined to the banks. Anyone reading the Leveson report into the phone hacking scandal will be shockingly aware that the ethical deficit in the Press is equally serious. Almost worse, those appointed to curb abuse—regulators, police, politicians and other public authorities—failed to act to deal with the abuses, turning blind eyes and deaf ears to the evidence showing just how pervasive the lax moral code has become. At the time of writing, the Jimmy Saville scandal is the latest, and probably not the last, example in this sorry tale. It is said of golf scores that 'how many' is more important than 'how', and that approach seems now to characterise many, if not most, areas of life. Pile up the profits, keep the share price high, boost your sales and outdo your rivals: how doesn't matter; its only how much that counts. We are confronted with the extent to which crude economic calculus has permeated all aspects of life. To quote Jane Collier again:

> The language of economics is the language through which the world is understood, the language by which human and social problems are defined and by which solutions to those problems are expressed. Our lives are dominated by the rituals of 'getting and spending'.[1]

The tragedy is that this dominance has been achieved in an individualistic age impatient of limitation, an age in which freedom is falsely equated with the absence of constraints, so that economic life has been cut free from the moral framework designed to ensure that it serves the common good. Perhaps it is only in such an age that this could have come about; but now we have to live with the consequences, and we have to ask if we are happy with the way things have turned out, and if not, we need to ask ourselves seriously what are we going to do about it. The contributors to this book are among those who are not happy; we have endeavoured to ask what can be done, and this book is the beginning of our answer.

At the heart of our answer is our conviction that the Christian faith has much to offer in regaining the ethical perspective that we have lost. We do not believe that there is 'a' distinctive Christian economic or political programme in contrast with secular or non-Christian ones,[2] but we do believe that there are Christian moral values that are essential to the working of a healthy economy, and that it is the task of the Church to call those with power and responsibility, both high and low and in all aspects of life, to work out for themselves what honouring those values requires them both to do, and personally to become.

First and foremost, we point to the need to recover a sense of virtue. We are, of course, not alone in making this point, but we do go further than some in pointing out that recovering virtue requires a change in ourselves, an acknowledgement that we are spiritual beings, and that if we ignore our spiritual nature we are diminished as people and we simply stack up more and more problems for ourselves. But making the connection between the personal and the economic is for many a step too far. We seem to have been persuaded that life can be lived in separate compartments: private and public, spirit and work, morality and business, religion and politics. This duality is as alien to Christianity as it was to the ancient prophets of Israel. As Andrew Lightbown points out in Chapter 1, the laws of Israel allowed no distinction between the sacred and the secular; God was to be honoured in the market place as much as in the holy place, business and trade are as much a part of worship as prayer and sacrifice. By dividing life into compartments we become divided people, and a divided life is an unfulfilled life; God wants us to be whole. I think many people recognise this, but acknowledging the proper place of religion is a step too far. Many prefer to say that they are spiritual rather than religious, and that is fine; but we suggest that this spiritual awareness needs to become more robust, rooted in the world, a shared resource, and not just a purely personal possession. The Christian faith challenges us to see the self that is active in business and commercial life as an expression of our spirituality as much as the self that is active in our private life. 'Spirituality' has many senses; understood in the way just described, our spirituality is more-or-less synonymous with character, those enduring marks or etched-in factors in our personality, including our inborn talents as well as our acquired traits imposed upon us by life and experience, which, in Al Gini's words, define us, set us apart, and motivate behaviour.[3] Spirituality is not an ill-defined feeling or dimension of life that exists on its own; it is always earthed in particular attitudes and values, and these can be secular as well as religious—indeed most spiritualities today are secular, and this is the heart of the problem. Secular spiritualities tend to be materialistic and self-centered; re-connecting economics and ethics requires a spirituality that transcends self, and that is why religion is part of the solution. If it is right that we are 'hard-wired' for God, then we need to keep our wiring in good condition. Faith has a role in re-connecting economics and ethics.

Alan Hargrave's essay describes the essence of a spirituality for our times based on the teachings of St Benedict. It is not surprising that Benedictine insights feature in other essays because St Benedict speaks in a voice particularly attuned to our times, and many in the business world, who would not describe themselves as religious, have found him a helpful guide. Benedict lived when the Roman Empire was declining into the 'Dark Ages', and a large part of his appeal is because history is repeating itself. The philosopher Alasdair MacIntyre argues that 'a crucial turning point in that earlier history' occurred when men and women of goodwill turned aside from the task of shoring up Roman power because they realised that the continuation of civility and moral community was not to be equated with the maintenance of the power and structures that made up the Roman establishment. 'What they set themselves to achieve instead', he says, 'was the construction of new forms of community within which the moral life could be sustained so that both morality and civility might survive the coming ages of barbarism and darkness.'[4] The monastic communities that St Benedict founded were instrumental in this process. They kept alive the Christian faith and values which underlie our European civilization—the morality and civility of which MacIntyre speaks—until the darkness dispersed. We face the same task today. MacIntyre is not the only one who senses that a new dark age is already upon us, and that the barbarians have already been governing us for some time. As he says, we await another—though doubtless very different—St Benedict.

To some this may sound alarmist, but underlying the economic and moral crises that beset us today is the gradual failure of the basic ideas that have sustained western civilization since the Enlightenment. The rise of Islam should alert us to this. Behind the militancy is a deeper protest that the ways of the West have not led to justice: the gap between rich and poor widens, the unrestrained quest for economic growth has depleted and polluted the earth's resources, and the failure to tackle climate change is making a bad situation worse. At root, the protest is against a system that excludes the insights of religious faith from public life. Writing in the immediate aftermath of 9/11, Scott Thomas pointed to this deeper dimension: 'What many in the Islamic world wish to safeguard—not just the fanatics—is the definition of religion as a community of believers, rather than a privatised body of beliefs.'[5] It is perhaps the loss of the understanding of the importance of faith as a foundation of community that is our greatest peril.

Faith teaches us that virtue is a communal possession before it is an individual possession. If the cardinal virtues are to be incorporated into our economic system, as Rowan Williams has suggested, then they need wide support in the community. For example, the concern for justice is universal, but justice is nothing if it is not a hallmark of the community; the community guarantees justice, but, with our loss of community our sense of justice has atrophied. Justice has come to be seen merely as a procedural requirement, and the economic theory that has developed since the Enlightenment is too concerned with processes and not sufficiently concerned with outcomes. Some economists equate justice with market outcomes, in effect deifying the market, believing that its outcomes are part of the natural order. This might be the case if all came to the market with equal power and resources, but they do not. Like any human institution, the market works in the interests of the powerful, and justice is sidelined. But there is no re-inventing the market; other economic approaches, like communism, simply do not work, and equally have failed to produce justice. We do not need a new mechanism; we need new values to control the way the only available mechanism works. The Christian faith contains these values, which are described in the first two chapters: humility and reverence, community, solidarity, justice, gift, service, and subsidiarity. They are, in fact, widely shared; we do not need to re-invent the wheel, but we do need to see their economic relevance. More importantly, though, we need to pursue them because they are right, because they make for human flourishing, and not because they will improve the economy. In other words, the time has come to stop shoring up the system simply because it is the system.

Alasdair MacIntyre looks for the formation of new forms of community to sustain our moral life. The different examples of a theonomic approach in this book may best be seen as examples of ways in which that new moral community might be formed—indeed is being formed—and new values brought to bear on the operation of the market. In each case a challenge is being made to accepted ways of doing things, and to the way we see ourselves. Each is about bridging the gap between the personal and the economic.

Ethical investment and charitable giving are perhaps the most widespread examples of new values taking root, and the fact that the criteria used for ethical investment are widely accepted—they are described by Frank Canosa as 'humanist' rather than Christian—shows that hopes for a wider ethical framework for the economy are not without foundation. Ethical investment can mean accepting lower returns, and this willingness to put others before self can be seen as expression of love, which, as we have said, in economic terms means taking everyone's interests seriously. The challenge is to make this mainstream, pursuing more wholeheartedly the path of positive discrimination in ethical investment, supporting companies that aim to trade responsibly and fairly rather than simply avoiding those whose activities are regarded as harmful or unjust.

Taking gift seriously exposes a lacuna in classical economic theory. Gifts comprise a major category of transactions, but classical economics struggles to explain altruism, even though it is one of the basic human motivations. The challenge here is clear: to reformulate the theory so that it reflects what actually happens. The new approach to economic theory called 'human economics' will hopefully offer a way forward.

Ethical investment and charitable giving are the expression of an inchoate moral community, though none the less effective because of that. More concrete is the community formed in the workplace, and in Chapter 9 Nick Bion illustrates the ethical values on which it is based. It is clear from what he writes that 'business ethics' is not necessarily an oxymoron, and that it is possible to be both fair, ethical and profitable. There is a sharp moral challenge in what Nick writes to our ideas about company ownership, pay and incentives. Nick's company rejects gross differentials in pay between boardroom and staff, and enables the staff to participate in the profitability of the enterprise along with the shareholders. The prevailing understanding of ownership and incentives is too narrow, and diminishes us as people; ownership is not about maximising the owners' rewards, nor are bonuses and other financial inducements the only incentives. Nick also poses a sharp moral challenge about tax. Community requires a shared commitment to the common good, and this is shown particularly in a willingness to pay tax, and, as Nick points out, this includes the corporate sector—a live issue as I write with the news that some major economic players (Starbucks, Google and

Amazon among them) pay little tax or no tax at all. There is a growing impatience with all forms of free-loading, whether it is tax avoidance, unjust differentials, or unjustified expenses. This feels to me like the beginning of a new form of community concerned to renew our moral sense 'so that both morality and civility might survive the coming ages of barbarism and darkness.'

Do we also see the emergence of new forms of community in the more difficult areas of social life where we seek to provide for those in need? Housing is one such area, and in Chapter 10 Keith Croxton shows clearly the difference a theonomic approach makes to intractable social problems. A moral community places need and justice above market power and profit maximisation, but, more importantly, it recognises that the problem is not solved simply when the houseless are housed, but when they have a home within a community. There are many challenges here. Our needs are not just material, but social and emotional also. Meeting these needs is part of the justice towards which economic outcomes should be directed, but they go unmet because we fail to see the poor as part of our community, and more deeply because, ignoring our spiritual nature, we do not think that it is part of the state's responsibility to meet these needs.

Schools are where the new form of community will be nurtured, and education is transformed when it is seen to be about forming a moral community as well as individual attainment. In Richard Backhouse's theonomic approach, children are treated as individuals and not as economic units. That, surely, is what every good parent wants, but education is being harnessed to suit the needs of the economy, and its wider social purpose is neglected. If Alasdair MacIntyre is right when he says the barbarians have been governing us for some time (and this was in 1981!), we need look no further for an example of barbarian rule. Again the challenges are many, but underlying them, as with all our examples, is the need to reverse the dominance of the economic model of life. This is persuasively argued by Owen Nankivell in his seminal study, *Economics, Society and Values*. He argues that the drive for more material goods, the pre-occupying concern for economic activity in western culture, means that we are putting the cart before the horse. Society is more than 'getting and spending', or, to paraphrase Jesus,[6] our life is more precious than our possessions: 'Society as a whole provides an over-arching context in which to set economic activity. If the consequences of the latter or the practice of particular values in the latter, conflict with wider social aspirations it is clear which should yield . . . Nevertheless, the presumption in western market capitalism appears to be that the economic model . . . drives and dominates peoples' lives . . . '[7] Theonomics is about putting the horse back in front of the cart! Human value comes before financial value, but because it is not measurable, in economic life it is subordinated. It is too easy to place people in categories according to their worth, or their worth to us. Harder, but more vital, is acknowledging the God-given equality of all. That, in the end, is what theonomics seeks to achieve.

NOTES

1. Jane Collier, 'Contemporary Culture and the Role of Economics' in Hugh Montefiore (ed.) *The Gospel and Contemporary Culture* (London: Mowbray, 1992).

2. One of those who have argued that there is not a distinctive Christian economics is John Sleeman. Writing in response to the economic crisis of the early seventies, he said, 'It emerges fairly clearly that there cannot be 'a' distinctive Christian economic or political programme to be contrasted with secular or non-Christian ones. Attempts in some countries to set up Christian political parties, or to advocate certain political views as being especially Christian ones, have only had the effect of discrediting the Christian faith by associating it with particular classes or interests, usually, in practice those of property or business. They have alienated from the church many sincere people who cannot accept the line of policy advocated, or who feel that the name of Christ is being invoked to support what they regard as

unjust or untrue'; see John F Sleeman, *Economic Crisis: A Christian Perspective* (SCM Press, 1976), p. 21.

3. Al Gini, 'Moral Leadership and Business Ethics' in Joanne B Ciulla (ed.), *Ethics, the Heart of Leadership* (Praeger; Westport, CT, 2004).

4. Alasdair MacIntyre, *After Virtue* (Duckworth, 1985), p. 263. Copyright © Alasdair MacIntyre. Reproduced with permission of Bloomsbury Academic, an imprint of Bloomsbury Publishing Plc.

5. Scott Thomas was writing in *The Church Times* (28.9.2001) in the aftermath of 9/11. He points out that, within Islam, there is a debate about the extent to which the state should be governed by Islamic law, as the protests and other events surrounding the referendum on the new Egyptian constitution shows. But even those who oppose moves towards establishing an Islamic State do not want to lose the social and moral framework that Islam provides for both public and private life. The debate is discussed by Gilles Kepel, *The War for Muslim Minds: Islam & the West* (Belknapp Press, 2004).

6. The paraphrase of Jesus is an attempt to catch the essence of that part of the Sermon on the Mount where he talks about material anxieties: see Matthew 6.19–34.

7. Owen Nankivell, *Economics, Society and Values* (Ashgate Publishing, 1995), p. 75.

Lightning Source UK Ltd.
Milton Keynes UK
UKOW03f2233170714

235290UK00001B/14/P

9 781908 381187